Using CAT Tools in Freelance Translation

This book explores the impact of applying computer-assisted (CAT) tools in freelance translation toward better understanding translators' strategies, preferences, and challenges in using new technologies and identifying areas of enhancement in translator training.

The volume offers a brief overview of the latest developments in technology in translation, examining such issues as the effect on the translation process and the dynamics of the translator-technology interaction. Drawing on data from a study with active translators in Poland, Pietrzak and Kornacki examine the underlying factors underpinning translators' lack of engagement with these tools, including such issues as prevailing preconceptions around technology and limited knowledge hindering the most efficacious use of these resources and the subsequent impact on translator identity. Taken together, the book brings together these insights to help pinpoint freelance translators' needs more effectively and adapt training programmes accordingly.

The volume will be of interest to scholars in translation studies with an interest in process and technology as well as active translators.

Paulina Pietrzak is Assistant Professor of Linguistics and, since 2008, has been affiliated with the University of Łódź, Poland.

Michał Kornacki is Assistant Professor of Linguistics, affiliated with the University of Łódź, Poland.

Using CAT Tools in Freelance Translation

Insights from a Case Study

Paulina Pietrzak and
Michał Kornacki

Routledge
Taylor & Francis Group

NEW YORK AND LONDON

First published 2021
by Routledge
52 Vanderbilt Avenue, New York, NY 10017

and by Routledge
2 Park Square, Milton Park, Abingdon, Oxon, OX14 4RN

Routledge is an imprint of the Taylor & Francis Group, an informa business

© 2021 Taylor & Francis

Library of Congress Cataloging-in-Publication Data
A catalog record for this book has been requested

ISBN: 978-0-367-64675-2 (hbk)
ISBN: 978-1-003-12576-1 (ebk)

Typeset in Times New Roman
by Apex CoVantage, LLC

Contents

Tables

Figures

Introduction

Overview of the Book

Since the advance of computer-assisted translation (CAT) tools, technology has exerted a significant impact on the translator's workflow. The book attempts to explore the technological evolution in translation and its effects on the process of translation. It offers a classification of translation technology and discusses various modes of translator-technology (TT) interaction. The authors delineate the profile of the contemporary freelance translator and advocate for the implementation of the "technological toolkit" (i.e., the basic set of instrumental skills and technical abilities related to information technology) in the translation classroom. Given that translation technology affects the translator's work style, the book touches upon the impact that TT interaction can exert on the translator's self-concept. It also discusses the notion of anxiety related to the use of translation technology.

The authors investigate the application of CAT tools in freelance translation and analyse how the actual usage and preferences differ among professional translators. With the aim of understanding the demographics and attitudes of freelance translators, a study has been conducted on both users and non-users of CAT software in Poland. Given the limited – yet to a large extent universal – scope of the study, the Polish context well illustrates why a great number of professional translators still refrain from using CAT tools, while others fail to use them efficiently or do not make use of all the features available to better address their clients' expectations. The findings of the study help to identify the needs of the translation market and improve strategies used in translator training.

The scope of the book is of immediate concern in the contemporary translation market encompassing rapid advances in translation technology. The findings demonstrated in the study help to determine the actual tendencies and mechanisms in the use of CAT tools. The analysis of the results elucidates the reasons for the apparent reluctance towards those tools in the freelance translation market and shows implications for both software developers and translator trainers. New insights on freelance translators' interaction with translation technology can contribute to the discussion on translators' IT skills and the need for facilitating the use of CAT tools in the translation classroom.

Introduction

Tremendous progress has been made in the development of state-of-the-art CAT software. Designed to improve productivity, CAT tools not only help in managing translation projects but also show potential for increasing translation quality and customer satisfaction. Over the past 20 years, there has been a significant rise in client demands for efficient and reliable translation service. Translation commissioners expect high-quality translation delivered in the shortest possible time, which makes CAT tools a necessity. Apparently, every contemporary translator employs some sort of technology in the translation process (hereinafter referred to as translation technology) on a daily basis. Nevertheless, the extent to which the translator interacts with technology differs considerably. Rapid changes in preferences and expectations of the translation market consequently lead to the need for altering the approach to CAT technology in the organisation of translator training.

The present book discusses the results of a study designed to explore the attitudes and preferences of freelance translators. The first chapter examines various forms of employment in the translation profession with a particular focus on the freelance translation market. The second chapter demonstrates the typology of translation technology and modes of translator-technology (TT) interaction. The third chapter discusses the competences and skills of freelance translators as well as the differences in the translators' profiles. Chapter four explores the key developments in CAT technology and their effects on the translator's work. Given the possible negative impact of CAT tools on the product and process of translation, it discusses the cognitive and metacognitive aspects of TT interaction. In chapters five, and six, and seven, the authors report the findings of a survey research carried out on professional translators working with various language pairs whose native language is Polish. The main assumption underlying the study is that, despite all the benefits of computer-assisted translation, the translation market remains divided into users and non-users of CAT tools.

1 Contemporary Freelance Translation Market

Overview of the Chapter

The translation market ecosystem is discussed here in the context of today's translation profession and industry growth. In this chapter we explore the dynamic nature of the contemporary freelance translation market and language market. The chapter covers official approaches to the profession of the translator in various countries and categorisation of the profession (section 1.1). An overview of various forms of employment in the translation profession is provided with particular focus on freelance translation approached from a demographic and sociological perspective (section 1.2). It is observed here that the surge of globalisation in the translation industry leads translators to increase their productivity. Since the demand for translation and the speed of delivery grows steadily, the industry recognises the value of technology and importance of using CAT tools in the translation workflow.

1.1 Freelance Translation as a Profession

Translation technology is now omnipresent in the translator's work, which simplifies and accelerates the process of translation. It is not only a great aid which helps the translator work efficiently but is also a factor which changes the face of the translation profession. New developments in translation technology (especially computer-based tools) stimulate changes in the workflow of the contemporary freelance translator. Long gone are the days when translation was associated with dictionary-based pen-and-paper work. Given the increasing reliance on technology to translate quickly and efficiently, the effects of technology result in the emergence of new types of work profiles and work systems.

As Cronin (2013: 8) states, "the potential instantaneity and accessibility of digital media imply a greater acceleration of translation flows with potentially subversive effects, but equally the widespread dissemination of translations."

Technological innovations have caused the freelance translation market to change so dynamically that it has become more diverse than it has ever been. Both economic and sociocultural aspects of globalisation have had a great impact on the condition of the translation business and the required skills for the position of a freelance translator. The translator's job is highly specialised and requires a number of qualifications (see Bell, 1991; Robinson, 1997; Gouadec, 2007) and competences (Kiraly, 1995, 2000, 2014; González Davies, 2004; Tennent, 2005; Hurtado Albir, 2007; Piotrowska, 2007; Klimkowski, 2015). Given that job requirements depend on the economic situation and growth of innovation in the translation industry, it is hard to identify the specific universal scope of work and duties for every translator.

The discussion on various forms of employment in the translation profession has to start with an attempt to show how big the translation market is. In a report dated 17 August 2009, the Directorate-General for Translation (DGT) of the European Commission estimated the language industry within the EU at 8.4 billion euro in 2008. The figure comprised "the industry sectors of translation, interpreting, software localisation and website globalisation, language technology tool development, language teaching, consultancy in linguistic issues and organisation of international conferences with multilingual requirements. In addition, it included language-related activities performed in corporate environments" (Rinsche and Portera-Zanotti, 2009: iii). Limited only to translation and interpreting (including software localisation and website globalisation), the market's worth was estimated at 5.7 billion euro in 2008 (ibid.: iv). The study predicted steady growth of its value. In fact, in 2019, the global market for outsourced language services and technology will reach 49.6 billion US dollars (DePalma et al., 2019). In fact, the global language service provision market has been growing steadily for the last decade and, considering globalisation factors in the economy, it is expected to continue to grow. The implication is that either there will be room for more professionals, or current language service providers (LSPs), especially translators, will have to optimise their workflow in order to offer faster, better, and, as a result, cheaper service.

While there are big language service providers on the market (CSA has recently published a list of 100 LSPs whose annual revenue for 2018 exceeded 7.5 million US dollars [CSA, 2019]), the core of the market is individual translators who perform most of the translating and post-editing work. The question arises here about the profile of the translator and occupations characterised as relating to the translation profession. According to the DGT (Pym et al., 2012: 17), in

the Statistical Classification of Economic Activities in the European Community (NACE) we find Translation and Interpretation listed as a separate category (74.3), alongside Specialised design activities, Photographic activities and Other professional, scientific and technical activities. This classification is picked up in some of the national listings (in Croatia, Poland, Portugal and the United Kingdom, for example) and in principle should apply throughout the European Union.

Such categorisation states that the profession of a translator, or interpreter, should be considered an independent entity, even if it is not fully regulated in some countries. In fact, little regulation regarding the profession is available. For example, the report states that in "no country that [has been] surveyed is any academic qualification – or indeed any kind of formal qualification at all – required in order to use the term 'translator' or its equivalent *generic* terms" (ibid.: 20). Some intergovernmental institutions regulate this precisely, even if there are no state regulations available. For example, the DGT hires translators with at least two foreign languages and "a university degree, not necessarily in languages" (ibid.: 21). There are guidelines developed to help specify standards of professional conduct, and some countries (e.g., France, Germany, Poland, Spain) require notarisation to authenticate legal translations. Nevertheless, in most cases, the only condition in order to be recognised as a translator is to declare translating on a commercial basis. As observed by Pym et al. (2012: 3), "the generic activity of translators appears not to qualify as a 'regulated profession' in terms of Professional Qualifications Directive (2005/36/EC): no one can stop an unqualified person from working as a translator." There is no statutory professional regulation that would determine the formal criteria necessary for becoming the translator.

1.2 Forms of Employment

Professional translation activities encompass various forms of employment, and there have been numerous attempts to categorise the profession (see Robinson, 1997; Gouadec, 2007; Pym et al., 2012; or Klimkowska, 2013). For instance, Gouadec (2007: 92–102) proposes a very detailed overview of the profession.

1. Salaried translators – according to Gouadec (2007: 92–102), "the salaried translator is bound to her/his employer" by a standard work contract and receives fixed salary for his/her work. This category is further divided into:

    a) In-house translators – translators who work in in-house translation departments of various companies or governmental/non-governmental organisations;

b) "Temping" – "to all intents and purposes, translators hired by 'temping' agencies work as freelancers, except that they are salaried employees and do not have to look for contracts themselves" (ibid.);

c) Translation company translators – in-house translators working full-time in translation agencies;

d) Agency staff – project managers who supervise translation projects (including freelance subcontractors) on a brokerage basis;

e) Translators under the umbrella company system – translators who conduct their business under the auspices of an umbrella company;

f) Special cases:

    i. The "on-site" translator – a translator employed by a company which outsources his/her services to another company. The translator provides his/her services on the client's company premises;

    ii. A translation outsourcing project manager – project managers who supervise translation projects (including freelance subcontractors);

2. Freelance translators – translators who usually are self-employed and provide translation services directly to clients or translation agencies;

3. Translators working for publishing companies – "translators working under the 'publishing industry' scheme may be literary translators, media translators and even localisers. Whenever applicable, they have in common that they are paid as authors" (ibid.);

4. "Outlaws" –"'translators" who work unofficially, thus not paying any taxes or other state-proscribed contributions;

5. "Invisible" translators – individuals who carry out the duties of a translator in the company they work in but are employed under a different job description (e.g., a secretary);

6. Special cases:

a) Second-job translators – individuals who do not consider translation to be their main occupation. Usually, they work in another profession (e.g., as a teacher or engineer) and consider translation as the opportunity to get extra income;

b) Part-time translators – "the part-time translator usually is a freelance or salaried translator who has decided to spend more time with wife (or husband) and kids and who incidentally belongs to a household with more than one income" (ibid.);

c) Occasional translators – individuals who translate only occasionally and do not consider translation as their occupation;

d) Remote translators – salaried translators who work from a remote location.

The categorisation proposed by Gouadec (ibid.) has been widely recognised and followed (sometimes with slight deviations – see, for example, Klimkowska, 2013), but it is too detailed for research purposes, so in the present book the focus is laid on a simplified division. The authors opt for the most remarkable division between in-house (or salaried translators) and freelance (or self-employed) translators in either full-time or part-time jobs. The research presented here (chapters 6–7) focuses on workers who consider translation to be the source of financial benefits. In fact, when closely considered, the categories proposed by Gouadec (2007) can be distributed amongst those two general categories:

1. **Freelance**

    a) freelancers
    b) translators working for publishing companies
    c) second-job translators
    d) part-time translators
    e) occasional translators
    f) remote translators

2. **In-house**

    a) in-house translators
    b) "temping"
    c) translation company translators
    d) agency staff
    e) "on-site" translators
    f) translation outsourcing project manager
    g) "invisible" translators

The division is based on the form of employment. The degree to which they are immersed in the profession is of secondary importance, especially if the translator is regarded as "an individual who translates for a living [regardless of whether it is full- or part-time] . . . and whose language skills have been verified by translation buyers" (Kornacki, 2018: 18).

Freelancers are translators who are either self-employed (more frequently) or take commissions based on a contract for specific work (less frequently) and work for, usually, two or more bigger LSPs or any other company that does not hire its own in-house translators. In-house translators are employed directly by companies to translate in-house content or translate in-house the content submitted for translation. In this case, the employer can be an LSP (a translation agency) or a company that is not involved in commercial language service provision but requires significant amounts of content to be translated to satisfy their own needs. Such translators are frequently bound by confidentiality and/or a non-compete clause which prevents them from working for other companies at the same time. Therefore, translators who are salaried employers with a fixed monthly salary fall into the "in-house" category (even in the case of "on-site" translators because services are provided on the client's premises). While "invisible" translators are not recognised as such, nevertheless they carry out the duties of an in-house translators and, therefore, fall within this category.

Translators working under the umbrella company system, which can take on many different guises,

> have a hybrid status. They are both freelancers since they set their own rates, find the translation contracts and remain in direct contact with the clients, and salaried employees of a company (i.e., the umbrella company), which will take care of all the administrative and legal paperwork on behalf of the translators.
>
> (Gouadec, 2007: 96–97)

Therefore, they are not listed in this category. "Outlaws," on the other hand, are not listed due to the fact that the category involves questionable practices of increasing one's own profits through tax evasion. It is our belief that the division is relevant with regard to the discussion of the profession in general, especially considering the fact that in-house translators can work as freelancers after their day job (to earn extra money).

Based on studies reporting the total number of freelancers in a given population, it can be argued that freelancers constitute the larger group. As summarised by Pym et al. (2012: 89), "weighted average [based on the mentioned studies] suggests that the general proportion of freelancers is around 78.4 percent." Taking into account the recent market growth trends, the number today is possibly even greater since it is no longer possible to house all the translators required to satisfy translation demands of bigger LSPs on the market. For example, in the case of the European Commission,

> more and more translations are now outsourced, both in pursuit of cost-efficiency and due to insufficient internal capacity. All in all, the number of in-house translators in the pre-enlargement languages has been reduced by almost 50 per cent over the last twenty years, but with the arrival of the new languages, the total number of translators in the Directorate-General for Translation (DGT) of the European Commission has remained roughly the same.
>
> (Strandvik, 2017: 124)

Considering sociological aspects of the profession, as reported by Pym et al., the freelancer is most likely a woman (three in four translators are female, 2012: 85) and a higher-education graduate who is either self-employed or working part-time. Their work is based primarily on short-term contracts carried out for several individual LSPs. The LSPs may include small and large companies but may be other freelancers as well. Self-employment gives the benefit of choosing specific contracts and shaping one's own translator workshop (e.g., one's own choice of the technology employed). Moreover, working for a number of different LSPs gives the opportunity to translate diverse content and develop one's own translator skills. At the same time, such freedom allows freelancers to specialise, also thanks to the use of specific translation tools or communication/file management software. Another benefit of being a freelancer is setting one's own timetable. Freelancers are limited in this respect only by the deadlines they have to meet. Otherwise, they set their own work times, which may be one of the reasons why it is so attractive to women who, theoretically, can mix their professional career with having children while staying at home (ibid.).

Freelancers principally use two modes of client-contractor interaction: direct and indirect. The direct one involves the client contacting the freelancer directly with the content to be translated. The freelancer produces a quote and translates the document if the quote and job conditions are accepted by both sides. The translation is delivered and paid for. The indirect mode involves the freelancer translating a job for an LSP (a translation agency). In this case, assuming that the freelancer has obtained an established cooperation agreement with the LSP, the only variable to be decided upon is the deadline (although frequently it is fixed, and the translator has the option to refuse the job if other assignments make it impossible to meet the deadline). The job is translated and delivered to the LSP. In most cases, the payment is based on a single invoice (listing all of the jobs assigned) generated at the end of the month. The LSP can be a translation agency or another freelancer who has accepted a direct contract that requires the assistance of other translators (for example, due to the volume of the job, a short deadline, or both), which works also on a greater scale, involving LSPs contracting several smaller LSPs, who in turn contract individual freelancers, to carry out bigger translation projects. Such job cascading requires meticulous planning and careful supervision, carried out by project managers on various levels of the project.

Cascading projects pose a challenge to all parties involved, freelancers included, since frequently they demand time as well as financial and **technological flexibility**. Technological flexibility is a psychological property that involves meeting technological prerequisites for the entire project (e.g., if the project involves CAT tool management with centralised resources (translation memories, termbases, context notes, and so on)); all subcontractors on all levels have to use the same tool, which basically means they have to know how to use it. Contrary to **technological anxiety** (see section 4.5.3), technological flexibility involves openness to accept new technological challenges, discover the means to face them, and successfully use the experience in the future. Given that the translation market becomes even more globalised day by day, there is a dire need for a pro-technological approach to the profession of a translator, which will be discussed later in the course of the book.

Globalisation is the main driving factor behind the translation market today. Combined, language service providers and freelancers are required to translate tens (if not hundreds) of millions of words day by day, exerting direct influence on diplomacy, tourism, trade, and culture. The demand for translation and the speed of delivery grows daily. True, not all of that is high-quality translation, as frequently merely a gist translation is needed, and such service can be provided by automated MT-based tools. This fact in itself shows that the volume of human translation today, while staggering, does not meet all of the demands of the market. The reason behind this situation is that, while the language service industry utilises technological advancements in order to improve efficiency and quality, individual translators do not follow suit. Don DePalma from the Chief Strategy Office at Common Sense Advisory notes that

> [w]e see a phenomenon in translation as it shifts from a cottage industry to a much more technology-dependent one, with large volumes of content flowing in many directions. . . . The data lead us to believe we are approaching a turning point, at which the language services industry will need to reinvent itself.
>
> (DePalma, 2012)

The problem that the industry has to face is the productivity of translators as opposed to market demand. In a report titled *Translation Future Shock*, the CSA provides the following summary findings, which picture the scale of the problem:

- The majority of translated content is new. How many words are "brand new" words, translated for the first time, without any use of translation memory software? The rate was 59.38% for translation companies and 59.11% for freelancers, which means that approximately 40% of content translated takes advantage of previous translation work.
- Translation productivity has stagnated. The report found that individual translators on average produce 2,684 words per day, while the average LSP reported a daily output of 43,546 words. The average LSP processes 5,728 words per hour, whereas freelancers translate an average

of 443 words hourly. The longstanding industry benchmark for translator output has been 2,500 words per day. Productivity increases have been minimal over the last decade.

• Many have tried machine translation. The survey also sought to determine the percentage of translation volume that was assisted by machine translation (MT) software. Less than half of translation companies (44.02%) and more than half of freelancers (55.00%) stated they had tried MT at some point.

(DePalma, 2012)

The report shows that, while over half of freelancers claim to have tried MT before (which can lead to the assumption that they use/have used CAT tools before as well), their overall average productivity has remained the same over the years. While such state of affairs is not a problem for individual translators (who have reached their maximum daily output), it is a problem for the global translation market. As was mentioned before, the demand for translation grows and has to be addressed properly. The solution to the problem can take either approach (or both): to train more translators or to reinvent the translator's workshop in order to increase productivity of freelancers (and LSPs, by extension). Considering the diversity of translators on the market (age, experience, computer literacy, the will to adapt), the second option alone may not be enough. It would be best to train new translators in the new fashion. Those new professionals could then gradually saturate the market, thus increasing overall productivity. The industry recognises the importance of CAT tools for the market and suggests higher education training centres also take them into account (see chapters 5–7 in this book). However, it is worth noting that the volume of texts waiting to be translated (and the fact that CSA found about 40% of content for translation may possibly take advantage of the previous translation work) suggests that CAT education should not be an option but a mandatory part of any translation course.

The following chapter discusses the use of technology in the process of translation. First, the typology of translation technology is delineated, followed by a short discussion on translator-technology (TT) interaction modes.

References

Bell, Roger. (1991). *Translation and Translating: Theory and Practice*. London: Longman.

Cronin, Michael. (2013). *Translation in the Digital Age*. London and New York: Routledge.

CSA. (2019). *The Largest Language Service Providers: 2019* [Online]. Available at: https://csa-research.com/More/Global-Market-Study/Top-100-LSPs (Accessed: 9 July 2019).

DePalma, Donald A. (2012). *Translation Future Shock*, pp. 16–18 [Private access per subscription. https://csa-research.com]. (Accessed: 9 July 2019).

DePalma, Donald A., Pielmeier, Hélène and O'Mara, Paul D. (2019). *The Language Services Market: 2019. 15th Annual Review of the Services and Technology Industry That Supports Translation, Localization, and Interpreting* [Private access per subscription. https://csa-research.com]. (Accessed: 9 July 2019).

González Davies, Maria. (2004). *Multiple Voices in the Translation Classroom.* Amsterdam and Philadelphia: John Benjamins.

Gouadec, Daniel. (2007). *Translation as a Profession.* Amsterdam and Philadelphia: John Benjamins.

Hurtado Albir, Amparo. (2007). Competence-based Curriculum Design for Training Translators. *The Interpreter and Translator Trainer*, vol. 1(2), pp. 163–195.

Kiraly, Don. (1995). *Pathways to Translation: Pedagogy and Process.* Kent: Kent State University Press.

Kiraly, Don. (2000). *A Social Constructivist Approach to Translator Education: Empowerment from Theory to Practice.* Manchester: St Jerome.

Kiraly, Don. (2014). From Assumptions About Knowing and Learning to Praxis in Translator Education. In: Piotrowska, Maria and Tyupa, Sergiy (eds.), *Challenges in Translation Pedagogy, Special Issue of Intralinea* [Online]. Available at: www.intralinea.org/specials/article/2100 (Accessed: 17 December 2019).

Klimkowska, Katarzyna. (2013). *Orientacja na sukces zawodowy studentów kończących studia translatorskie.* Lublin: Wydawnictwo UMCS.

Klimkowski, Konrad. (2015). *Towards a Shared Curriculum in Translator and Interpreter Education.* Wrocław and Washington, DC: WSF, PAN and International Communicology Institute.

Kornacki, Michał. (2018). *Computer-assisted Translation (CAT) Tools in the Translator Training Process.* Berlin: Peter Lang.

Piotrowska, Maria. (2007). *Proces decyzyjny tłumacza. Podstawy metodologii nauczania przekładu pisemnego.* Kraków: Wydawnictwo Naukowe Akademii Pedagogicznej.

Pym, Anthony, Grin, François, Sfreddo, Claudio and Chan, Andy L. J. (2012). *The Status of the Translation Profession in the European Union* [Online]. Available at: https://termcoord.eu/wp-content/uploads/2013/08/The_status_of_the_translation_profession_in_the_European_Union.pdf (Accessed: 9 July 2019).

Rinsche, Adriane and Portera-Zanotti, Nadia. (2009). *Study on the Size of Language Industry in the EU* [Online]. Available at: https://publications.europa.eu/en/publication-detail/-/publication/9a68479a-1c07-4c43-8d1a-8d49782c0808 (Accessed: 9 July 2019).

Robinson, Douglas. (1997). *Becoming a Translator: An Accelerated Course.* London: Routledge.

Strandvik, Ingemar. (2017). Evaluation of Outsourced Translations: State of Play in the European Commission's Directorate-General for Translation (DGT). In: Svoboda, Tomáš, Biel, Łucja and Łoboda, Krzysztof (eds.), *Quality Aspects in Institutional Translation.* Berlin: Language Science Press, pp. 123–137. https://doi.org/10.5281/zenodo.1048194

Tennent, Martha (ed.). (2005). *Training for the New Millennium: Pedagogies for Translation and Interpreting.* Amsterdam and Philadelphia: John Benjamins.

2 Application of Technology in the Process of Translation

Overview of the Chapter

Translation technology is a vital force that aims primarily to support the work of the translator. It is a system of digital tools employed by freelancers (or LSPs in general) in professional translation. One of the more valued aspects of translation technology in widespread use today is computer-assisted translation (CAT). However, before a discussion on the application of CAT tools can commence, what needs to be illustrated is the scope of translation technology (section 2.1). This chapter outlines previous approaches to translation technology and proposes a typology based on the translation type in which the tools are used (regular translation, audiovisual translation, and interpreting) and considered from a freelance perspective. The chapter also explores various forms of translator-technology (TT) interaction (section 2.2) that can be distinguished in the translation process. Five levels of TT interaction are outlined in an attempt to show what degree of affinity with CAT technology is required from the translator to build a successful career.

2.1 Typology of Translation Technology

The authors will now discuss the main types of what can be considered translation technology to illustrate the scope of CAT technology. So far, there have been several attempts to propose a more or less accurate typology. As can be assumed, the notion is broad and poses a challenge when trying to define it. So far, there have been several attempts to propose a more or less accurate typology. Hutchins and Somers (1992) focus their attention on machine translation. Indirectly, they outline differences between different types of technology utilised in translation based on the level of automation involved. In their discussion, they refer to machine-aided human translation (MAHT) and human-aided machine translation (HAMT). While they agree that "the central core of MT itself is the automation of the full translation process," they also accept the role of the human translator in the process (post-editing in HAMT/MT or the use of MT in MAHT/CAT). Thus, the first type of typology presented here is based on the degree of human involvement in the translation process.

Another approach, proposed by Enríquez Raído and Austermühl (2003), differentiates between "translator tools," which allow translators to unfold their creative potential, and "localiser tools," which are meant to manage the business of translation, both at a local and global level. Table 2.1 depicts in detail how tools are distributed in this typology.

The model proposed by Enríquez Raído and Austermühl (2003) has aged well. The clear division into individual and business is still valid, even if blurred nowadays. Considering the current state of affairs, both in terms of the requirements of the translation market and the technology available, more and more translators also become translation company managers (even if it is an individual enterprise) and are required to know and use localiser tools. While the authors agree that such tools as encyclopaedias or specialised websites and newsgroups are still reserved mostly for individual translators and their preferences, they cannot say the same about quality assurance (QA) tools or machine translation engines. These have become

Table 2.1 A typology of translation and localisation technology

Translation and localisation technology			
Localiser/productivity tools		Translator/knowledge tools	
DTP tools	Term extractors, termbases	Termbases (glossaries)	Encyclopaedias
Quality assurance tools	Translation memories *back end*	Translation memories front-end	Dictionaries
Project management tools	Localisation tools *back end*	Localisation tools *front end*	Digital archives
Workflow systems			DIY corpora
Content/ globalisation management systems			Concordances
Machine translation			Specialised websites and newsgroups
Internationalisation tools			Multilingual knowledge management

Source: Enríquez Raído and Austermühl (2003) [italics by the authors]

easily accessible (through CAT tools), and their use is frequently not only expected but required (Doherty, 2016).

What is more, the authors have taken the liberty to italicise "front/back end" in the case of translation memories to signal that they do not fully agree with the statement that translation memories back ends (understood here as off-CAT MT creation and editing) are available only to localiser companies. More and more translators see the need and benefit of having robust translation memories that can be used for any project in the future. At the same time, the authors recognise the fact that translation memories (TMs), while important to maintaining "phraseological and terminological consistency and thus translation quality" (ibid.: 8), may hamper the creative potential of an individual since they promote speed and efficiency of translation, which is achievable only in the case of repetitive content that leaves scarce (if any) room for creativity.

The authors start with those two typologies here due to the fact that the first one shaped our perception of translation technology as MT and, partially, CAT related, while the second one introduced the key problem of "who does what" and what tools are involved in the process. A number of attempts at categorisation of computer tools used in translation (e.g., Melby, 1982, 1998; Alcina, 2008) have been made since then. Some of them give foundations for key concepts in computer-based translation (see, for example, Melby, 1994, 1998; Hutchins, 1999–2009). The most recent categorisation that the authors of the book were able to access is the Nimdzi Technology Atlas,[1] presenting current software distribution on the translation market. It presents a very detailed typology of translation technology available on the market as of the year 2019. In this case, translation technology is divided into six main branches, each with a number of sub-branches:

1. Translation tools

   a) Workflow systems

      - LSP business management
      - Localisation for developers
      - Proxy and JavaScript website localisation
      - TMS for LSPs and buyers
      - Buyer-only TMS from vendors
      - CMS middleware
      - Internationalisation

   b) Components

      - Translation editors
      - Terminology management

- TMX editors
- AutoQA
- Review

2. Interpreting tools

   - Interpreting scheduling
   - Remote interpreting apps
   - Conference interpreting apps
   - Speech recognition
   - Wearables

3. Media localisation

   - Project management
   - Dubbing tools
   - Subtitle translation

4. Machine intelligence

   - Production platforms
   - Natural language understanding

5. Machine translation

   - Ready-to-use
   - Adaptive
   - MT aggregators
   - Build
   - Niche

6. Marketplaces and platforms

   - Platform LSP
   - Data and terminology
   - Marketplaces

This particular typology takes into account all possible areas in which translation-related tools are used. As can be seen, its complexity is much greater than in the case of the typology proposed by Enríquez Raído and Austermühl (2003), although the changes are still rather evolutionary than revolutionary. It seems that the nature of the market (high degree of globalisation, very strong influence of modern, translation-oriented IT solutions) makes it impossible to determine a stable typology of all the tools used in translation which will remain valid for any longer period of time, especially if one considers the fact that most of the tools available on the market at the moment are under constant development and overlap a number of categories of tools (see the example of SDL or SmartCat, as pictured in the Nimdzi's Language Technology Landscape, 2019). In order to address that issue, the authors of the book propose a different type of categorisation of translation technology based on two principles:

a) type of translation that the tools are used for, and
b) a freelancer perspective.

Therefore, the authors have decided to break the translation technology into three categories: regular translation, audiovisual translation, and interpreting. Regular translation is, in turn, divided into word processors, CAT tools, machine translation, content management systems, translation management systems, and graphics software. Audiovisual translation features three subcategories: AVT tools, Assistive Technology, and localisation tools. The last category, interpreting, is further divided into video remote interpreting, bring-your-own device interpreting, interpretation management systems, and automatic interpreting (see Figure 2.1). The tools are grouped into three subsets. However, their use is not limited exclusively to one subset. Combined, they constitute the authors' perspective on technological tools employed by professional freelancers.

This division is explained in detail later in the chapter. The authors acknowledge previous studies on the issue which have led to these developments; it is their hope, however, to discuss the complexity of translation

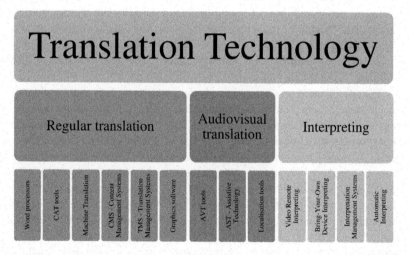

Figure 2.1 Typology of translation technology

technology from the freelancer's perspective. The following paragraphs outline each category, with more emphasis placed on regular translation since its subcategories are more directly related to the actual CAT technology and, thus, are the main focus of the book.

2.1.1 Technology in Regular Translation

The first set of tools to be presented within the scope of this typology are tools used in the regular (or "written") translation. It has to emphasised here that the authors do not mention workflow, globalisation management systems, or internationalisation tools per se. We believe that the framework established by Enríquez Raído and Austermühl (2003), and further expanded by Nimdzi, is valid and the "localiser" aspect can still be considered in terms of those. We aim to offer more specific typology based on tools that are in actual use by contemporary freelancers. This part of the typology received the most attention since it concerns (in)directly the problem of CAT tools in freelance translation. Additional attention was paid to machine translation since we believe that after being apart for many years, CAT and MT tools are closer than ever, possibly even on a course to become one tool to support human translators in their everyday work.

2.1.1.1 Word Processors

A word processor tool is a computer programme used to type, format, and store text. The *format* aspect is very important here since translation has to follow the visual form of the original, and the adequate text formatting is critical. Therefore, the authors of the book consider such tools as MS Word, Libre Office Writer, or Apple's Pages as examples of word processors, while text editing tools like MS Notepad are to be considered text editors.

The use of word processors is so widespread these days that hardly any people take a moment to reflect upon their importance in translation. In most cases, it is the word processor software that is used to open and visualise content for translation and render target text accordingly. "[D]espite the fact that CAT tools and machine translation solutions do receive more and more recognition, word processors still constitute an unshakable foundation of a translator's workshop" (Kornacki, 2018: 49). In the contemporary digital market, the word processor is the most basic tool that the translator needs to be able to translate. Thirty years ago, translators would still use pen and paper to do translations; the widespread use of personal computers shifted this tendency to a computer (word processor) and a translation printed on paper. Easy access to the Internet changed the market even further, allowing documents to be sent and received in a digital form; hence the position of the word processor as the basic tool for translators.

What is more, it has to be noted that by the very nature of word processors, they are frequently the source and target medium for translations done using machine translation or in CAT tools; for example, source PDF files can be translated directly in CAT tools. There is, however, a high risk of faulty target layout of the document. Therefore, PDF files are often converted to DOC/DOCX file format, translated, exported back to DOC/DOCX, checked for layout consistency, and saved back to PDF if such is the requirement of the client.

2.1.1.2 CAT (Computer-Assisted Translation) Tools

A CAT tool is a computer programme that assists the human translator in the process of translation by allowing instantaneous access to various linguistic and text editing/formatting assets. The assets are integrated into the same translation environment (Kornacki, 2018).

> The core of CAT tools is a translation memory (TM), a computer database that stores a translator's translated text alongside its original source text, so that these pairs can later be reused in full or in part when the translator is tasked with translating texts of a similar linguistic composition.
>
> (Doherty, 2016: 950)

Apart from TM, CAT tools offer translators access to termbases (custom dictionaries), concordances, quality assurance and spellchecks, as well as machine translation. They have been designed to "improve translator's accuracy and productivity" (Kornacki, 2018: 107).

The origins of CAT tools date back to the Automatic Language Processing Advisory Committee (ALPAC) report, which discredited the viability of investing time and money in machine translation, allowing researchers to focus on corpus-based and statistical research, which contributed to the development of computer-assisted translation tools. The first proto-CAT tool was developed by Automated Language Processing Systems (ALPS) in the mid-1980s. It was named Translation Support System. Nevertheless, technological limitations and a poor user base made it difficult to develop this type of software further. The first tool to achieve commercial success "was Trados – thanks to successful European Commission tender bids in 1996 and 1997 – that found itself the tool of choice of the main players, and, thus, the default industry standard" (Garcia, 2015: 70). During the initial stage of CAT tools development, a wide range of new features were added. "By the end of the 1990s, such features as translation memory, alignment tools, terminology management and various file processing filters were available in the most robust systems" (Kornacki, 2018: 103). The trend has shifted, however, and nowadays few new features are added. Instead, software developers focus on refining the existing features, making them more effective and user-friendly (e.g., AdaptiveMT in SDL Trados or Machine Translation Quality Estimation (MTQE)[2] in the case of Memsource). The goal of those changes is to assure that the tools produce more accurate translation suggestions considering a given context.

In most cases, the development of these tools is governed by actual translators' needs and clients' expectations. A good example here is cloud computing. Recent years have been a witness to the emergence of cross-platform tools like Memsource, Wordbee, XTM Cloud, MateCat, or SmartCat. The problem with CAT tools was that they were Windows-bound (i.e., they required the MS Windows environment to run). It was, and often still is, a huge problem to macOS and Linux users who virtually have no access to state-of-the-art CAT tools. In order to address the problem, several companies have independently developed their own cloud solutions – CAT tools that are not installed on a computer but work online through a web browser in the Software as a Service (SaaS) model.[3] Those tools are practical examples of cloud computing[4] used for the benefit of the translation industry.

Currently, more and more CAT tools are evolving beyond mere translation tools. Instead, they are becoming translation platforms, a term denoting an "all-in-one" software that enables the translator to translate using TMs, TBs, MT, and concordances, as well as create and edit TMs and TBs, and manage clients and projects (including such aspects as quoting, payment tracking, or project archiving; see Memsource for example). As a result, freelancers may focus on one primary CAT tool, using secondary ones when needed.

2.1.1.3   Machine Translation (MT)

The notion of machine translation has become more and more popular among the wider audience thanks to such online tools as Google Translate or Microsoft Translator. The term denotes a type of translation which is carried out automatically, without human intervention in the actual process.

The idea to have a machine translate for humans is not new. While one can note 17th-century dreams about translating machines (Hutchins, 2010), it was in the 1930s when a Russian scholar, Petr Troyanskii, formulated basic principles for a modern study on machine translation.

> [Troyanskii] envisioned three stages of mechanical translation: first, an
> editor knowing only the source language was to undertake the "logical"

analysis of words into their base forms and syntactic functions; secondly, the machine was to transform sequences of base forms and functions into equivalent sequences in the target language; finally, another editor knowing only the target language was to convert this output into the normal forms of his own language. Troyanskii envisioned both bilingual and multilingual translation.

(Hutchins, 2010: 434)

However, his insights generated little attention in academic society, mostly due to the fact that his impact was almost exclusively limited to Russia. In the West, the real progress on MT was initiated by Warren Weaver's memorandum in 1949. "Weaver suggested the application of cryptography, statistical methods, Claude Shannon's information theory and exploiting the logical features of languages" (Kornacki, 2018: 95). It has led to a number of ideas and events that expanded and supported MT. Abraham Kaplan of the Rand Corporation suggested a statistical approach to machine translation (Bar-Hillel, 1960). In 1952 the first MT conference was held at the Massachusetts Institute of Technology (MIT). One of its conclusions was that

a public presentation of a working MT system was needed in order to attract funding. Such presentation was held on 7 January 1954 at Georgetown. The demonstration – an MT system used to translate a pre-selected sample from Russian to English, basing on a closed set of 250 words and a few grammar rules – attracted a great deal of attention. The presented quality of translation assured substantial funding in the USA, as well as new MT projects blossoming around the world.

(Kornacki, 2018: 95)

However, there was a major flaw in the approach to MT at the time. People believed the primary goal of MT research was to create a fully automated high-quality translation system (FAHQT) capable of producing translations of equal quality to the human translator. The current level of thought and technology made it utterly impossible at the time, however. This has led to the creation of the ALPAC, which published a report on MT in 1966. The report claimed that "MT was slower, less accurate and twice as expensive as human translation and that there is no immediate or predictable prospect of useful machine translation" (ALPAC, 1966: online). The report heralded a stop in MT research for some time, advocating the theoretical and practical development of computer-based aids for translators (e.g., automated dictionaries). All was not lost, however, and some researchers continued working on MT, leading to such breakthroughs as Météo, employed to translate Canadian weather forecasts in 1976, French TITUS, Chinese

CULT, Japanese ATLAS, SYSTRAN, Xerox Corporation in-house MT, and an MT system developed by the Logos Corporation (see Hutchins, 2010). "Numerous solutions and successes fuelled extensive research on MT. The development of computers and new research in computational linguistics allowed to create new forms of data processing, like corpus-based or statistical machine translation" (Kornacki, 2018: 97). All of those achievements ensured the continued existence of machine translation on the market. Continued research has led to the following typology of MT:

- **Rule-based MT (RBMT)** – one of the very first MT strategies ever developed. "More complex than translating word to word, these systems develop linguistic rules that allow words to be put in different places, to have different meaning depending on context, etc." (Costa-Jussà et al., 2012: 248). RBMT can be broken into transfer-based, interlingual, and dictionary-based machine translation. Regardless of the type, RBMT incorporates grammatical, lexical, and stylistic rules to translate text between languages. The system is easy to maintain, but the volume of rules, as well as the time and linguistic knowledge required to build an RBMT system, make it very expensive to use. Apart from that, any rule refining introduced into the system is not guaranteed to increase its overall accuracy (ibid.).
- **Statistical (SMT)** – SMT utilises statistics to retrieve linguistic MT data (patterns and rules) from numerous large corpora. SMT systems depend heavily on the number of resources. Modern systems analyse phrases (building blocks in the case of the SMT) and produce translations "using the overlap in phrases" (Costa-Jussà et al., 2012: 249). The sheer volume of data that has to be processed in order to produce an acceptable translation (processed in real time) makes the system heavily computer-resource dependent. Hence, SMT systems require significant computational power (SYSTRAN, 2019).
- **Example-based (EBMT)** – first proposed by Nagao (1981), it is based on the idea of analogy. The system uses a corpus with already-translated texts which then is used as a source of sentences that contain matching sub-sentential components (Somers, 1999). These sentences are used to translate sub-sentential components from the source and into the target text. When combined, these phrases result in a complete translation.
- **Hybrid MT (HMT)** – a combination of RBMT and SMT (and more recently, NMT). A classical hybrid system processes the source text in one of two ways:
  - "translation is done using the rule-based system, and then the output is adjusted with the help of the statistical system, or

- rule-based system is employed to pre-process a source text, then an SMT system translates it, and finally the RBMT system takes over again in order to adjust the output" (Kornacki, 2018: 99).

Such hybridisation results in better translation quality, flexibility, and control. Less data to train the software and less computing capacity are also required (SYSTRAN, 2019).

- **Neural MT (NMT)** – an evolution of SMT. NMT uses artificial neural networks[5] to predict sentence structure (i.e., word sequence), creating a single integrated model. Instead of being phrase-based, like in a regular SMT, NMT is based on a sequence of words, predicted one at a time (Wołk and Marasek, 2018). The predictions are based on the source and already-translated target word sequence. In fact, this is one of the core advantages over SMT systems. An NMT system does not require any external "specialised systems" utilised by SMT. Instead, it can be trained directly on the source and target text. Bahdanau et al. (2014: online) explain that "[u]nlike the traditional phrase-based translation system which consists of many small sub-components that are tuned separately, neural machine translation attempts to build and train a single, large neural network that reads a sentence and outputs a correct translation." Wu et al. (2016, online) follow this, saying that "[t]he strength of NMT lies in its ability to learn directly, in an end-to-end fashion, the mapping from input text to associated output text." However, the training process is by no means fast and requires huge amounts of input. Together with "ineffectiveness in dealing with rare words, and sometimes failure to translate all words in the source sentence" (ibid.), they constitute the three core areas for improvement of the NMT (see also Goodfellow et al., 2016; Goldberg, 2017).

All of the aforementioned systems types are in use today and are successfully employed, depending on the individual needs of the companies that utilise them. However, it appears that most of the MT systems available to the general audience through the Web seem to be either neural or hybrid MT systems.

The application of MT in freelance translation takes two approaches: the use of MT services through a web browser and via APIs (application programming interfaces) built into contemporary CAT tools.

In the first instance, a translator can refer to a website that provides a front end of an MT service (e.g., DeepL, Amazon Translate, Microsoft Translator, or Google Translate) and use a search engine to request an automated translation of any sentence. Such an approach has its pros and cons. The fact that frequently such a service can be used for free is undeniably an advantage.

While not all services offer a "free mode," translators still have a variety of choices. When discussing the disadvantages of such solutions, it has to be acknowledged that using MT services over the Web is not the fastest way to benefit from the automated translation. A translator has to copy and paste the content for translation, again copy and paste the translated text into the translated document, and modify the translation if need be. In such a case, it may be worth considering the use of CAT tools and MT API instead. The solution poses a challenge since one has to know (and own a licence) how to use CAT tools to benefit from such an approach.

Contemporary CAT tools employ MT in various forms (mostly as plugins which assist translators by providing TM match-like suggestions of translation), although the main principle of machine-aided human translation (MAHT) is retained. Teixeira (2011: 108) stresses the difference between translation memory systems and machine translation systems. He

> distinguishes translation memory systems from machine translation systems. . . . TM systems show translators the "provenance" and the "quality" of the translation suggestions coming from the memory, whereas MT systems display the "best translation suggestion possible" without any indication of its origin or degree of confidence.

The second statement has started to become obsolete since more and more CAT developers have introduced MT-quality estimation tools (e.g., Memsource's MTQE), which try to show the "MT match quality." As Doherty (2016: 953) observes, MT systems are "continually improving in terms of their quality and efficiency as their infrastructures become more refined and more high-quality translation data become available." The worth of MT integration into CAT tools can be seen when there are no results from translation memory, and the translator has to resort to his own skills. MT plugin connects directly to the service via an API and requests translation of a given segment of text. The translation is then inserted into the target segment for the translator to evaluate and confirm (once satisfied with its quality). The entire process, except for the proofreading stage, is done automatically in seconds. The downside of this approach is that in order to use API, one usually has to use a paid version of an MT service (e.g., access to API in DeepL requires a subscription of 19.99 euro per month (as of May 2020) as opposed to the free version over the web browser).

Some freelancers mention another issue common to both approaches. The problem concerns the confidentiality of the data translated with the use of MT systems. The documents the freelancers translate frequently fall within the scope of non-disclosure agreements. Moreover, while there are MT providers who declare that the data is removed from the system after being processed (e.g., DeepL, paid account), this is not always the case. Novović (2017) discusses the issue of broad licence terms on the Web, bringing the example of a clause modelled closely on terms offered by Google in 2016 (for reference see Novović, 2017: 216):

> When you upload, submit, store, send or receive content to or through our Services, **you give us** (and those we work with) **a worldwide license to use,** host, store, reproduce, modify, create derivative works (**such as those resulting from translations,** adaptations or other changes we make so that your content works better with our Services), communicate, publish, publicly perform, publicly display and distribute such content. The rights you grant in this license are for the limited purpose of operating, promoting, **and improving our Services,** and to develop new ones.
>
> Novović (2017: 202)[6]

The passage presented here implies that any content uploaded to an online service, including MT service, can be used by the provider. It can be assumed that "improving our Services" implies that the text translated in MT Web engines will be used only to train the neural network behind the engine in order to make it better. However, unless stated otherwise, it cannot be claimed that the data is not stored for an indefinite period of time by the service provider. What is interesting, the problem mentioned earlier is not restricted to Web MT tools. For example, when setting an MT engine in memoQ, the following is displayed in a dialog box (memoQ 9, 2020):

> The source text will be sent to an external provider. If the text contains personal data, you may not be allowed to send it, according to GDPR and national data protection regulation. Please check the Privacy Policy and the Data Processing Agreement offered by the provider. If they have a signable Data Processing Agreement, please sign it.

The content of the dialog box is obviously a safety measure meant for freelancers working with MT plugins. It suggests that not all MT service providers remove the data after it is processed. One can speculate that this is the case because the data is used, again, to train the neural MT networks. While the reasons behind the process are understandable, the act itself can be regarded as questionable from the point of view of the company who owns the text in the first place.

This suggests that it is not always the case that MT can be used. While it is easier and faster to use it together with CAT tools, ultimately the nature of the text and individual arrangements with the client validate its use.

2.1.1.4   *CMS – Content Management System*

A content management system is a software application (or a set of applications) used to create and modify digital content. There are two types of CMS: a) enterprise, designed for closed workgroups (a collaborative environment, including document and digital asset management, as well as record retention among others); and b) web, designed for website design and management (adding and editing online content, including graphics, media, and computer codes).

A typical CMS has two main components: front-end user interface (UI) which allows users to add, modify, and remove content with no need for programming skills, and back end which allows users to modify the structure of the website, add/remove new features, and edit the actual HTML code of the published content. CMSs are very versatile thanks to the use of themes (visual aspects of the website) and plugins, which extend the functionality of a base CMS (e.g., galleries, online payments, databases, and more). According to W3Techs,[7] as of September 2019, the most widely used CMS is WordPress (61.4%), with Joomla and Drupal coming in second (4.9%) and third (3.1%), respectively.

While CMSs are not translation tools in themselves, most of them can use plugins which help to translate the content published via those CMSs (e.g., WPML, TranslatePress, or Polylang). The translation process can take place within the CMS environment (a translator needs to have access to the back end) or outside of it. The translation outside of the CMS can take two forms:

a)   the content is extracted by the website administrator, delivered to the translator, translated, sent back, and then published by the administrator. The process is complicated and requires much manual work. The advantage is that the third party (the translator) does not get access to the back end of the CMS, which may be unwelcome due to security reasons;

b)   a special CAT tool plugin is installed in a CMS (e.g., Memsource plugin for WordPress[8] or Drupal), which enables a translator (or translation agency) to check website updates in real time, download new content, and translate it shortly after it is published. Once the translation is complete, it can be delivered straight to the CMS for publication.

Both options require a relatively high level of technical affinity and familiarity with the technical requirements of the job on the part of the translator (or project manager) since they need to react to the individual needs accordingly and warrant customer satisfaction.

2.1.1.5 TMS – Translation Management System

The idea behind a TMS is to have a computer system that will help to automate the translation process. Since the primary aim of the system is to benefit translator efficiency, this category can be conceived of as basically the same as CAT tools. The difference, however, lies in the scope of those two notions. CAT tools' role is specifically focused on facilitating the translation process and boosting translation quality through increased cohesion of target documents. TMSs, on the other hand, go beyond to utilise CAT tools and process management to facilitate data flow, speed up projects through collaborative working, and keep track of all the data.

A TMS can be used in many ways. LSPs use it to allow their clients to add content to the translation (e.g., through the use of Automatic Project Creation and connectors in Memsource), manage the entire process, and deliver the final project semi-automatically. The same takes place in the case of software developers who offer multilingual software solutions and use a TMS (thus also becoming LSPs) in order to increase cost efficiency.

The use of a TMS is limited for freelance translators, mostly due to the costs involved.[9] Most of the contemporary CAT tools include at least a rudimentary TMS, which allows users to manage individual projects, translation memories, and termbases. There are also tools which offer additional features (e.g., project management, TM, TB, and MT sharing, as well as collaborative work – Memsource) as part of the basic subscription plan. While less of an advantage for translators who work mainly for translation agencies, the option may have a significance for those freelancers who work directly for the final customer, delivering top-quality translation services.

2.1.1.6 Graphics Software

Apart from the tools mentioned previously, two additional tools that freelancers frequently use, to a lesser or larger extent, are optical character recognition (OCR) tools and graphic editors. Both allow users to process graphics from the translator's perspective. OCR software allows users to convert a scanned image which contains a text into a form that is machine-readable (through a process of pattern matching) and save it as an editable file (Bowker, 2002: 26). Since CAT tools require editable files, translators who use CAT tools in their workshop frequently need OCR software in order to convert non-editable documents (or non-editable sections of otherwise editable documents) into text content that can be imported into CAT tools. The use of OCR calls for a number of technical skills, the most important of which involves the ability to analyse the document and decide whether it is "suitable for conversion, what problems the converter may find and how to address them (before, during and after the process)" (Kornacki, 2018: 50). While technically OCR is an example of text conversion software, it has been listed in the *graphics software* subcategory since frequently the source document is an image (graphics), so the conversion process should be seen as graphics to text rather than text to text.

Another tool that can prove useful in freelance translation is graphic editing software. Following the idea proposed by Pym (2013) that the translator is a language service provider, what needs to be taken into consideration is the extent of this service provision. Sometimes translators have to deal with elements which cannot be altered from within a word processor or a CAT tool (e.g., brochures, posters, static Internet content, and so on) due to the fact that clients often expect translators to provide full service (Pym, 2003; Risku et al., 2016) and translate a source text in PDF, JPG, PNG or TIFF formats (just more popular examples) like a regular translatable file (e.g., DOCX, ODT). When confronted with such a task, the freelancer has two options: either to outsource the graphic-editing part of the job to a DTP (desktop publishing) professional, or carry out the editing on their own (requires knowledge of such software as Adobe Photoshop, CorelDRAW, Inkscape, and Adobe Illustrator, for example). Kornacki (2018: 51) shows that both options have their advantages and disadvantages (Table 2.2).

Table 2.2 Advantages and disadvantages of outsourcing graphic editing

Translators outsource graphic editing	*Translators edit graphic source themselves*
Advantages	**Advantages**
• No need for sophisticated skills • No need for specialised software • Time saved on editing can be used for other pure translation projects	• Full control over content modification • The translator keeps entire remuneration • Full control over the overall progress of the project development and deadlines
Disadvantages	**Disadvantages**
• Risk of errors in the final document as most DTP (desktop publishing) specialists are not language professionals and may not be proficient in source/target language • Part of the total remuneration is spent on DTP services • Translators have to depend on the time and skills of third parties, which may have an influence on the final deadline.	• Need to acquire specialised skills and software, some of which can be very expensive • DTP is time-consuming

Source: Kornacki (2018: 51)

Table 2.2 shows that while graphic editing is not an essential skill for a successful freelancer, and outsourcing may prove to be more time-efficient, at least rudimentary knowledge of the tools and the process may prove to be useful in the long run – even if it is only to be used for DTP error correction.

2.1.2 Technology in Audiovisual Translation

In short, audiovisual translation (AVT), or multimedia translation, deals with the translation of audiovisual content. Despite the primary association of AVT with film translation, this type of translation service "has expanded to include sitcoms, animated productions (including cartoons), documentaries, commercial clips, corporate video material and (partially) video game localisation" (Bogucki, 2019: 9). In the case of AVT, even more than in the case of regular translation, freelancers have become subcontractors, providing language services to AVT companies who have the tools, frequently company-tailored software, that enable them to deliver state-of-the-art translation products. In fact, many companies like Netflix, Amazon, or computer game developers hire freelancers themselves and have them use their own systems and frameworks, thus becoming direct language service managers and buyers. Such companies offer their own tools to freelancers in order to uphold maximum coherence for entire projects.

2.1.2.1   AVT vs AST Tools

There is, however, a wide range of tools available to freelancers who work on their own and complete individual AVT projects. Those tools can be divided into two groups: AVT tools and Assistive Technology (AST). AVT tools include software that allows for regular subtitling (e.g., open-source Subtitle Edit or commercial EZTitles), as well as some CAT tools tailored to AVT (e.g., memoQ via the use of AVT plugins and filters), subtitling for the deaf and hard-of-hearing (SDH), and audio description (AD) for the blind and partially sighted audiences. AST tools include computer programmes that assist both the translator in the process of audiovisual translation (e.g., speech recognition software) and the target audience in accessing online content (e.g., blind and partially sighted audiences – screen reading and magnification of content; deaf and hard-of-hearing – speech recognition). Please refer to Bogucki (2019) or Bogucki and Deckert (2020) for more comprehensive reflections on AVT.

2.1.2.2   Localisation Tools

A separate category of translation tools that the authors have decided to include in the AVT section is localisation. Esselink (2003: 21) states that "in a nutshell, localization revolves around combining language and technology to produce a product that can cross cultural and language barriers. No more, no less." The widely used term "localisation" is, in fact, a popular name for two distinct processes (i.e., internationalisation and localisation). Internationalisation involves the process of designing a computer programme in such a fashion that it can be adapted, or translated, to foreign languages, regions, and cultures without the need to introduce structural changes. Localisation, on the other hand, describes the process of adaptation of digital content (software)[10] for a specific culture, language, or region through translation. It needs to be noted that the process of localisation may be undertaken on both internationalised and non-internationalised software. The two options differ heavily in the number of resources that have to be involved in the process (non-internationalised software being more demanding in this respect). Therefore, freelancers less commonly become involved in solo localisation projects (with the exception of website localisation when the freelancer has considerable IT skills). It is more likely for them to participate in collaborative projects where they are responsible for the linguistic aspect of the endeavour, namely the translation. Therefore, translators would either use regular CAT tools which offer coherence both in terms of style and terminology, or they are asked to work with software that is tailored to suit the needs of individual localisation companies. The potential use of CAT tools is an aspect shared with *regular translation tools* (see section 2.1.1); however, the authors decided to include localisation in the AVT section due to the nature of the translated content.

2.1.3   Technology in Interpreting

With miniaturisation and new advances in mobile devices, new technologies have made it possible for interpreters to work remotely, delivering their services to a wide array of devices (smartphones, smartwatches, tablets) in real time. Modern interpreters have access to a number of different technological solutions, which can be grouped into four general categories.

VIDEO REMOTE INTERPRETING (VRI)

VRI allows interpreters to work from home or provide interpreting services for call centres. VRI reduces or eliminates travel costs for interpreters and, depending on the type of service, allows users to charge per minute instead of per hour or translation bloc. Therefore, VRI is most appropriate in situations when short interpreting sessions are required (e.g., business meetings or medical appointments). The technology involved is predominantly web-conferencing software. In many cases, it offers basic functionality for free, while more advanced features are available for a fee. Examples of such software include Interprefy, Interpreter, Headvox, Voiceboxer, or Akkadu (Nimdzi's Language Technology Landscape, 2019), to name a few.

BRING-YOUR-OWN-DEVICE INTERPRETATION (BYOD)

BYOD is a type of interpreting where the only interpreting equipment necessary is a broadcasting device (e.g., interpreter's mobile device) and receivers (e.g., personal smartphones with a respective free app installed which allows access to the interpreting broadcast). It is an easier and cheaper solution for the organising party. Examples of the software include, for example, Headvox. There are also systems that combine remote interpreting with an ability to transmit to mobile apps. These are called Interpreting Delivery Platforms (IDPs).

INTERPRETATION MANAGEMENT SYSTEMS (IMSS)

Interpretation Management Systems, akin to translation management systems, are used to manage projects. They allow users to organise interpreting jobs/bookings and collect feedback on translation quality. They are too costly to be used by individual freelancers and are employed primarily by LSPs and other companies that have to manage large numbers of interpreting jobs. Examples of such tools include thebigword, Pancea, Fluency, Plunet, or lango.

AUTOMATIC (SPEECH-TO-SPEECH) INTERPRETING

Automatic interpreting, also called "machine interpreting," allows translators to translate speech to speech without the need for a human interpreter. The principle behind it is that a voice recognition system recognises speech and converts it to text, which is in turn processed by an MT engine. The output text is then synthesised to speech using a text-to-speech (TTS) system. While automatic interpreting may seem to be the future of interpreting, it depends heavily on the following factors:

a) environment (no or muted background sounds) and speaker (clear standard accent) when converting voice to text;
b) machine translation engine quality (which in turn depends on good source quality);
c) quality of the TTS system.

Nevertheless, many companies have undertaken attempts to create automatic interpreting services (e.g., Google, Amazon, Wordly).

A recent addition to the world of interpreting, computer-aided interpreting (CAI) fits partially into this category. CAI systems feature voice recognition (Speech-to-Text) and machine translation systems to provide the interpreter with real-time assistance (see, for example, Fantinuoli, 2018) (e.g., translating vocabulary) during interpreting sessions.

2.2 Translator-Technology (TT) Interaction Modes

The contemporary translator interacts with the computer so extensively that they can almost be called an inseparable pair. The work of the translator is "determined by internet searches, glossaries, spell checkers, grammar checkers, translation memory and machine-translation databases, and anything else resembling a communication technology" (Pym, 2011: 4). Nowadays, apart from the regular use of the computer, there are also computer-assisted translation (CAT) tools easily available on the market. Introduced in the 1990s by SDL company, CAT tools make this interaction even more complex and, thus, potentially challenging. CAT tools are considered to "play such a central role in professional translation processes that translators can be assumed to be less in charge than they used to be, which may mean that translators are being pushed towards the periphery of the translation profession" (Bundgaard et al., 2016: 106).

The translator's interaction with technology is multifaceted and divergent. The translator's interaction with technology (as presented in the typology of translation technology – see Figure 2.1) can probably take as many possible forms as there are translators. However, the authors have decided to limit the scope of this book to the aspects of regular translation[11] related to CAT tools. Therefore, they suggest the typology of the translator's interaction with translation technology demonstrated in sections 2.2.1–2.2.5 on the basis of the extent to which they employ technological tools in translation.

2.2.1 Basic TT Interaction

The first and very basic type of interaction is the classical three-step form of translation, which involves receiving the source text, transferring information, and formulating the target text. "The network- and computer-based resources used during this core translation process aim at providing the translator with the linguistic, encyclopedic, and cultural information necessary to successfully perform his or her task" (Enríquez Raído and Austermühl, 2003: 225). In short, this type of interaction involves the use of computers and the Internet to produce a translation. Translators use such tools as word processors and digital (online and offline) dictionaries.

2.2.2 Extended TT Interaction

This type of interaction involves a greater dose of technological flexibility to deal with immediate problems, like document conversion and advanced text formatting (Kornacki, 2018) (i.e., using a word processor to the fullest extent in order to address any formatting challenges posed by the OCR (conversion errors) and clients (special needs regarding the layout of the document, usually paid extra)). Advanced text formatting involves, but is not limited to, page settings (e.g., section breaks, headers and footers), forms, macros, object positioning, and layering. During extended TT interaction in the process of translation, translators conduct more intensive research online and use such resources as message boards, social networks, corpora, and concordances (outside CAT tools).

2.2.3 CAT-Inclusive TT Interaction

In this type of interaction, the regular translation still occupies the first and largest part of the process. However, translators do occasionally use CAT tools to carry out single projects that benefit from the use of CAT software. It can be assumed that they do not require CAT tools (lack of CAT-specific jobs[12] or a price tag – see our research results presented in chapter 6) and use them as free software.

2.2.4 CAT-Based TT Interaction

In contrast to the previous type of interaction, here CAT-based interaction is taken to be the basic mode of translation. A translator owns a licence for one or more CAT tools and is familiar with a few more (in the case of projects which require licence sharing). All translations are conducted using CAT, with TM and TB resources shared between different tools. What is more, translators use advanced optical character recognition software to prepare documents to be translated in the CAT environment.

2.2.5 Full TT Interaction

In the most extreme form of interaction, translators make full use of CAT tools and their features, including concordances, alignment, regular expressions, and MT, to manage their entire workflow (quoting, job processing and delivery, job subcontracting, and so on). In this case, the entire translation workflow is CAT-oriented.

Translators are experienced individuals who understand all the pros and cons of this mode of translation. Those translators who are fully immersed in CAT philosophy have intimate knowledge of any linguistic limitations they force upon a translator and choose their jobs accordingly, having superior translation quality in mind. They know how to utilise various resources, including MT engines. In fact, as O'Brien and Moorkens (2014: 132) put it, in MT-assisted translation, translators switch between editing TM matches and post-editing MT matches. They conduct external reviews of translations done by other professionals (review/proofreading) and conduct post-editing of pre-translated documents (Bentivogli et al., 2016).

As was stated before, there can be as many forms of interaction as there are translators. Our aim here was to propose a distinction which takes into account the degree to which certain tools may be used in translation, as is partially shown in the results of our study. Not everyone uses CAT tools, and not everyone needs to use them. The use or non-use depends solely on the translator, his/her individual character, professional experience, and future professional needs. We believe that the typology presented earlier takes those aspects into account, resulting in a relatively precise framework.

Notes

1. Nimdzi's Language Technology Landscape v. 2019.07. Available online at: www.nimdzi.com/language-technology-atlas-2019/ (Accessed: 23 July 2019).
2. Machine Translation Quality Estimation (MTQE) is a feature of the Memsource CAT tool which identifies high-quality machine translation suggestions, reducing translation costs (Memsource, 2019).
3. SaaS means that the provider can use "applications running on a cloud infrastructure. The applications are accessible from various client devices through either a thin client interface, such as a web browser (e.g., web-based email), or a program interface. The consumer does not manage or control the underlying cloud infrastructure including network, servers, operating systems, storage, or even individual application capabilities, with the possible exception of limited user-specific application configuration settings" (Mell and Grance, 2011: 2).
4. Cloud computing is a model for enabling ubiquitous, convenient, on-demand network access to a shared pool of configurable computing resources (e.g., networks, servers, storage, applications, and services) that can be rapidly provisioned and released with minimal management effort or service provider interaction (Mell and Grance, 2011: 2).
5. "Neural network, a computer program that operates in a manner inspired by the natural neural network in the brain. The objective of such artificial neural networks is to perform such cognitive functions as problem solving and machine learning. The theoretical basis of neural networks was developed in 1943 by the neurophysiologist Warren McCulloch of the University of Illinois and the mathematician Walter Pitts of the University of Chicago" (Zwass, 2019).
6. Bold by the authors.
7. W3Techs is a "division of Q-Success Web-based Services. [Their] goal is to collect information about the usage of various types of technologies used for building and running websites, and to produce and publish surveys that give

insights into that subject. [The] company has no affiliation with any of the technology providers" (W3Techs: online).

8. Requires WPML.
9. Since proper TMSs are developed for companies which process huge amounts of data (frequently TMSs are customised to suit individual needs of the buyer), their price is usually of an order of magnitude higher than in the case of regular CAT tools. Some examples of TMS developers include SDL, Memsource, SAP, Across, XTM, or Lignotek.
10. The term "software" includes websites as well. Websites contain a computer code which is rendered into a website on the recipient computer system, which agrees with the definition provided by the Cambridge dictionary (https://dictionary.cambridge.org/dictionary/english/software) (i.e., "the instructions that control what a computer does").
11. Some of those can be used successfully in audiovisual translation.
12. In this context, "job" is understood as a translation assignment under a commercial order by an external client.

References

Alcina, Amparo. (2008). Translation Technologies Scope, Tools and Resources. *Target*, vol. 20(1), pp. 79–102. https://doi.org/10.1075/target.20.1.05alc

Automatic Language Processing Advisory Committee (ALPAC). (1966). *Language and Machines: Computers in Translation and Linguistics*. Washington, DC: National Academy of Sciences. Available at: www.mt-archive.info/ALPAC-1966.pdf (Accessed: 25 March 2019).

Bahdanau, Dzmitry, Cho, Kyunghyun and Yoshua, Bengio. (2014). *Neural Machine Translation by Jointly Learning to Align and Translate* [Online]. Available at: https://arxiv.org/pdf/1409.0473.pdf (Accessed: 31 May 2020).

Bar-Hillel, Yehoshua. (1960). *The Present Status of Automatic Translation of Languages: Advances in Computers*. Vol. 1 [Online]. Available at: www.mt-archive.info/Bar-Hillel-1960.pdf (Accessed: 27 August 2019).

Bentivogli, Luisa, Bertoldi, Nicola, Cettolo, Mauro, Federico, Marcello, Negri, Matteo and Turchi, Marco. (2016). On the Evaluation of Adaptive Machine Translation for Human Post-Editing. *IEEE/ACM Transactions on Audio, Speech, and Language Processing*, vol. 24(2), pp. 388–399. https://doi.org/10.1109/TASLP.2015.2509241

Bogucki, Łukasz. (2019). *Areas and Methods of Audiovisual Translation Research*. 3rd revised ed. Berlin: Peter Lang.

Bogucki, Łukasz and Deckert, Mikołaj (eds.). (2020). *Handbook of Audiovisual Translation and Media Accessibility*. Basingstoke: Palgrave Macmillan.

Bowker, Lynne. (2002). *Computer-aided Translation Technology: A Practical Instruction*. Ottawa: University of Ottawa Press.

Bundgaard, Kristine, Christensen, Tina P. and Schjoldager, Anne. (2016). Translator-Computer Interaction in Action: An Observational Process Study of Computer-aided Translation. *Journal of Specialised Translation*, vol. 25, pp. 106–130.

Costa-Jussà, Marta R., Farrús, Mireia, Marino, Jose B. and Fonollosa, José A. R. (2012). Study and Comparison of Rule-Based and Statistical Catalan-Spanish MT Systems. *Computing and Informatics*, vol. 31, pp. 245–270.

Doherty, Stephen. (2016). The Impact of Translation Technologies on the Process and Product of Translation. *International Journal of Communication*, vol. 10, pp. 947–969.

Enríquez Raído, Vanessa and Austermühl, Frank. (2003). Translation, Localization, and Technology: Current Developments. In: Gonzalez, Luis P. (ed.), *Speaking in Tongues: Language Across Contexts and Users*. València: Publicacions de la Universitat de València, pp. 225–250.

Esselink, Bert. (2003). *The Evolution of Localization. Guide to Localization. Multilingual Computing and Technology*. Archived from the original on 2012–09–07 [Online]. Available at: https://web.archive.org/web/20120907235057/http://isg.urv.es/library/papers/Esselink_Evolution.pdf (Accessed: 4 October 2019).

Fantinuoli, Claudio. (2018). *Interpreting and Technology: The Upcoming Technological Turn*. Berlin: Language Science Press.

Garcia, Ignacio. (2015). Computer-aided Translation Systems. In: Chan, Sin-wei (ed.), *Routledge Encyclopedia of Translation Technology*. Amsterdam and Philadelphia: Routledge, pp. 68–87.

Goldberg, Yoav. (2017). *Neural Network Methods in Natural Language Processing (Synthesis Lectures on Human Language Technologies)*. San Rafael, CA, USA: Morgan & Claypool.

González Davies, Maria. (2004). *Multiple Voices in the Translation Classroom*. Amsterdam and Philadelphia: John Benjamins.

Goodfellow, Ian, Bengio, Yoshua and Courville, Aaron. (2016). *Deep Learning (Adaptive Computation and Machine Learning Series)*. Cambridge, MA: MIT Press.

Hutchins, John. (1999). *Compendium of Translation Software* [Online]. Available at: www.hutchinsweb.me.uk/Compendium.htm (Accessed: 16 July 2019).

Hutchins, John. (2010). Machine Translation: A Concise History. *Journal of Translation Studies*, vol. 13(1–2), pp. 29–70.

Hutchins, John and Somers, Harold. (1992). *An Introduction to Machine Translation*. London: Academic Press Ltd.

Kornacki, Michał. (2018). *Computer-assisted Translation (CAT) Tools in the Translator Training Process*. Berlin: Peter Lang.

Melby, Alan. (1982). Multi-level Translation Aids in a Distributed System. In: Horecký, Jan (ed.), *Proceedings of Coling 1982*. Amsterdam: North Holland.

Melby, Alan. (1994). The Translator Workstation. In: Hammond, Deanna L. (ed.), *Professional Issues for Translators and Interpreters*. American Translators Association Scholarly Monograph Series VII. John Benjamins, pp. 127–149.

Melby, Alan. (1998). *Eight Types of Translation Technology* [Online]. Available at: www.ttt.org/technology/8types.pdf (Accessed: 16 July 2019).

Mell, Peter and Grance, Timothy. (2011). *The NIST Definition of Cloud Computing*. Gaithersburg: National Institute of Standards and Technology: U.S. Department of Commerce [Online]. Available at: https://nvlpubs.nist.gov/nistpubs/Legacy/SP/nistspecialpublication800-145.pdf (Accessed: 21 July 2019).

memoQ. (2020). *Computer Program*. Available at: https://www.memoq.com/ (Accessed: 23 July 2020).

memoQ. (2020). CAT Tool Developed by Kilgray, Budapest, Hungary.

Memsource. (2019). *Memsource Translate* [Online]. Available at: www.memsource.com/features/memsource-translate/ (Accessed: 21 July 2019).

Nagao, Makoto. (1981). A Framework of a Mechanical Translation Between Japanese and English. In: Elithorn, Alick and Banerji, Ranan (eds.), *Artificial and*

Human Intelligence: Edited Review Papers Presented at the International NATO Symposium on Artificial and Human Intelligence. Amsterdam: Elsevier Science Publishers. B.V., pp. 173–180.

Nimdzi. (2019). *Nimdzi's Language Technology Landscape v. 2019.07.* [Online]. Available at: https://www.nimdzi.com/language-technology-atlas-2019/ (Accessed: 23 July 2019).

Novović, Miloš. (2017). User-Generated Content: How Broad Licensing Terms Threaten the Web. In: Taddeo, Mariarosaria and Floridi, Luciano (eds.), *The Responsibilities of Online Service Providers.* New York: Springer International Publishing AG, pp. 201–217.

O'Brien, Sharon and Moorkens, Joss. (2014). Towards Intelligent Post-Editing Interfaces. In: Baur, Wolfram, Eichner, Brigitte, Kalina, Sylvia, Keßler, Norma, Mayer, Felix and Ørsted, Jeannette (eds.), *Proceedings* of the *XXth FIT World Congress.* Berlin: Bundesverband der Dolmetscher und Übersetzer e.V., pp. 131–137.

Pym, Anthony. (2003). Redefining Translation Competence in an Electronic Age. In Defence of a Minimalist Approach. *META*, vol. XLVIII(4), pp. 481–497.

Pym, Anthony. (2011). What Technology Does to Translating. *Translation & Interpreting*, vol. 3(1), pp. 1–9.

Pym, Anthony. (2013). Translation Skill-Sets in a Machine-Translation Age. *Meta*, vol. 58(3), pp. 487–503. https://doi.org/10.7202/1025047ar

Risku, Hanna, Pein-Weber, Christina and Milošević, Jelena. (2016). "The Task of the Translator": Comparing the Views of the Client and the Translator. *International Journal of Communication*, vol. 10(2016), pp. 989–1008.

SDL. (2020). *SDL Trados Studio. Computer Program.* Available at: https://www.sdltrados.com/ (Accessed: 23 July 2020).

SmartCat. (2020). *Computer Program.* Available at: https://www.smartcat.com/ (Accessed: 23 July 2020).

Somers, Harold. (1999). Review Article: Example-based Machine Translation. *Machine Translation*, vol. 14, pp. 113–158.

SYSTRAN. (2019). *What Is Machine Translation?* [Online]. Available at: www.systransoft.com/systran/translation-technology/what-is-machine-translation/ (Accessed: 28 August 2019).

Teixeira, Carlos. (2011). Knowledge of Provenance and Its Effects on Translation Performance. In: Sharp, Bernadette, Zock, Michael and Jakobsen, Arnt Lykke (eds.), *Human-Machine Interaction in Translation.* Frederiksberg: Samfundslitteratur, pp. 107–118.

Wołk, Krzysztof and Marasek, Krzysztof. (2018). Neural-based Machine Translation for Medical Text Domain. Based on European Medicines Agency Leaflet Texts. *Procedia Computer Science*, vol. 64, pp. 2–9.

Wu, Yonghui, Schuster, Mike, Chen, Zhifeng, Le, Quoc, V., Norouzi, Mohammad, Macherey, Wolfgang, Krikun, Maxim, Cao, Yuan, Gao, Qin, Macherey, Klaus, Klingner, Jeff, Shah, Apurva, Johnson, Melvin, Liu, Xiaobing, Kaiser, Łukasz, Gouws, Stephan, Kato, Yoshikiyo, Kudo, Taku, Kazawa, Hideto, Stevens, Keith, Kurian, George, Patil, Nishant, Wang, Wei, Young, Cliff, Smith, Jason, Riesa, Jason, Rudnick, Alex, Vinyals, Oriol, Corrado, Greg, Hughes, Macduff and Dean, Jeffrey. (2016). *Google's Neural Machine Translation System: Bridging the Gap between Human and Machine Translation* [Online]. Available at: https://arxiv.org/pdf/1609.08144.pdf (Accessed: 31 May 2020).

3   Freelance Translator Profile

Overview of the Chapter

In this chapter, the profile of the contemporary freelance translator is discussed with respect to changes that it undergoes. What used to be considered a tedious pen-and-paper job now appears to be a profession which takes numerous forms, oftentimes interactive, multimodal, and collaborative. The work of the translator, regardless of their use of CAT tools, is nowadays highly automatised, beginning from communicating with clients and translation agencies to organising stored documents and files. The translator's workstation combines access to various glossaries, dictionaries, and other terminological resources. Apart from that, the translator uses a range of additional devices from spell checkers and scanners, through web-based applications and OCR software, to translation memories and machine translation. Given the variety of forms of freelance translation and modes of TT interaction (section 2.2), the concept of translator competence differs significantly among freelance translators and is highly dependent upon the pattern and extent to which they use translation technology. The concept of translator competence is explored here (section 3.1) in relation to freelance translation and technological skills that allow translators to handle computer hardware and software in translation service provision (section 3.3). The chapter introduces the division into CAT users and CAT non-users (section 3.2) and discusses the characteristics and work styles of each group.

3.1   Freelance Translator Competence

It is hardly feasible to operationalise the concept of the contemporary freelance translator and thus their pertinent competence because nowadays there are wide discrepancies between translator profiles. As observed by Enríquez Raído and Austermühl (2003: 228), "today, translators find themselves in a diversified, automated, and highly professional working environment.

As experts for intercultural technical communication, modern translators often double as technical writers, lexicographers, software testers, or cultural consultants." Differences between two freelance translators can be observed not only in their specific tasks and responsibilities but also in daily work routines, work stations, methods of translating, ways of researching information, means of communicating with clients, and even job standards, interpretations of their job duties, or their own self-concept. In the case of every translator, all of those aspects differ to an unrecognisable extent, so the competence behind the use of technology is unique to a particular translator.

The ability to interact with the computer has become an important component of the translator's competence. Given that the contemporary translator's work is nowadays done utterly on the computer, it is quite common to come across technical difficulties. The job of the translator often means struggling with various system errors, programme installations, Internet connection errors, software incompatibilities, and so on. If such problems occur in the process of translation and prevent them from task completion, some translators can suffer frustration (see section 4.5 on anxiety).

The ability to interact with technology and face technical difficulties is a component of translator competence acknowledged among the skills listed and analysed in models of translator competence, albeit under different names. For instance, PACTE (2003, 2005) lists bilingual sub-competence, extra-linguistic sub-competence, knowledge about translation, and instrumental sub-competence with strategic sub-competence placed in the central part of the model as it controls all the other sub-competences. Here, technology-related competence falls under the category of translator's instrumental sub-competence, which involves "predominantly procedural knowledge related to the use of documentation sources and an information and communication technologies applied to translation: dictionaries of all kinds, encyclopaedias, grammars, style books, parallel texts, electronic corpora, searchers, etc." (PACTE, 2003: 59).

Kiraly (2000) refers to these types of skills as "translator-relevant computer competence"; it needs to be emphasised, however, that computerisation is not the only base for application of technology in the translation process. Although technology is associated with computers and their development, the coverage of the term is much broader. For instance, interpreters who work with conference equipment (mounted in an interpreting booth), voice transmitters (whispered interpreting, tours) or simply a telephone or a microphone, make use of technology that is not computer-related. Gil and Pym (2006: 5) mentioned that "[t]echnology extends human capacities. The monkey uses a stick to get a banana, and that stick is technology, in this case a simple tool. More general technologies are collections of tools." The implications of this claim suggest that any and all translator skills required to use electronic tools and equipment in the translation process be named translator technological competence.

The very term technological competence is used by EMT Expert Group (2009), who describe it as a sub-competence in the area of technology (2017). The European Master's in Translation (EMT) model considers this ability to be an element of a multi-componential model of translator competence labelled as 'technology (tools and abilities)' which "includes all the knowledge and skills used to implement present and future translation technologies within the translation process. It also includes basic knowledge of machine translation technologies and the ability to implement machine translation according to potential needs" (2017: 9).

Although "technology will always be one or two steps ahead of any multicomponential list" (Pym, 2003: 493), it is worth illustrating the scope of skills involved in the technological competence of the contemporary translator. What needs to be emphasised here is the practical aspect of technological competence. Translator technological competence involves developing skills that allow translators to handle computer hardware and software in translation service provision. Therefore, the technology-related translator competence model can thus be visualised as:

- basic computer handling (e.g., storage devices; input and output components, Internet connection, maintenance functions, and so on)
- text-processing (e.g., formatting, creating documents, lists, columns, etc., inserting images, tables, and the like, printing, and so on)
- e-mail based communication (e.g., presenting a quote to a client; processing orders; processing complaints; establishing a strong business relationship with the client)
- use of online sources (e.g., terminology, machine translation, online file converters, and so on)
- handling various file formats (e.g., identifying file extensions and opening software; document conversion)
- DTP and graphic software (e.g., redrawing diagrams and charts)
- use of CAT systems (e.g., translation memories, termbases, server projects, CAT revision tools, machine translation)
- localisation software (e.g., software and web localisation)
- use of AVT software (e.g., subtitling software)
- handling optical character recognition (OCR) systems (e.g., document preparation for computer-assisted translation)
- quoting of documents (e.g., processing character-, line-, or word-count; CAT-based document analysis and pricing)
- marketing (e.g., e-mail marketing, social media marketing, Customer Relationship Management (CRM) software, Content Management Systems (CMS), and so on)

- company management (e.g., invoicing, accounting software, spreadsheets, communication and collaboration tools, and the like)
- use of specialised interpreting-related equipment (interpreting booths, audio transmitters and receivers, and so on)
- use of other equipment (digital and non-digital) that may be needed during a specific translation/interpreting job (e.g., projectors, screens, other audio devices).

This model of translator technological competence encompasses skills that enable freelance translators to work as broadly defined language service providers. Still, not all of these skills are necessary for every translator, so the list is neither conclusive nor exhaustive. Given all the differences in the work styles of contemporary translators, their approaches to CAT tools also differ. As some translators cannot imagine working without the aid of computer-based technology, others still decide not to use it, which causes a division of the freelance translation market into users and non-users of CAT tools.

3.2   Users and Non-Users of CAT Tools

With cloud-based services and greater connectivity, CAT tool features become more and more convenient and easily available. Given the potential benefit of those tools, they could be expected to greatly facilitate every translation workflow; however, freelance translators are still divided into two groups, the users and non-users of CAT tools. Following the types of translator-technology (TT) interaction (see section 2.2), the levels of TT interaction can vary to a large extent. The translator's use of the computer can be very basic (2.2.1) when it is used mainly for writing and managing basic office work. In contrast to the workflow of the translators who limit themselves to online resource tools and corpora (see 2.2.2) or translators who sometimes use CAT technology (see 2.2.3), those who decide to use it on a daily basis (2.2.4 and 2.2.5) can be described as much more technology-reliant.

Such divergent forms of translator-technology interaction result in major differences in job characteristics. As stated by Pym (2011: 2), translators who work with external translation memories

> probably go faster, but not always; they probably get richer terminology, albeit at the expense of missing details like punctuation and cohesion markers; and they might confess, if working on a juicy text, that they spend proportionally longer mulling over the key translation problems.

Work styles differ even more, considering the fact that the coming of CAT tools have simplified the work of the translator who operates on text domains with recurrent lexical and syntactical characteristics. The translator who recurs to the use of CAT tools does not have to conduct similar researches repetitively since CAT tools automatically go through their previously translated content and the translator can use the segments suggested by their translation memory, thus capitalising on the repetitions and saving a lot of time and effort.

Nevertheless, CAT tool users differ within their own group as they use various tools. Therefore, their work styles differ as well. For instance, a lot of CAT tool-related problems are no longer a burden for translators who decide to use cloud-based services offered by cloud platforms such as Memsource. The main advantage of cloud-based services over desktop solutions is the fact that the data are safely stored and backed up. Moreover, such services operate from a web browser, so there is no need for installing any software in order to begin using the programme. Consequently, the user does not have to update the software, which happens to be problematic in the case of desktop solutions since it incurs additional expense and hinders the translator's workflow.

Problems that contemporary translators encounter differ even more, considering that the group of CAT tool users remains divided when it comes to their opinion on and the application of automation in translation. Depending on their stage of TT interaction (from sometimes to always; see sections 2.2.3–2.2.5), they may have different approaches to machine translation and the controversies around the use of MT technology. As Hutchins (1997: 115) observes, "in general most commentators agree that MT (full automation) as such is quite inappropriate for professional translators. They do not want to be subservient to machines; few want to be revisers of poor quality MT output." As Vieira (2018) found out in a study on translators' stance on machine translation, most grievances are "based on business practices themselves" and "most criticisms of MT are rooted not in fears of being outperformed by MT systems, but rather in the technology's limitations and market consequences." Nevertheless, translation technology tends to encourage automatic translation.

Machine translation (MT) technology has been integrated into CAT systems which now allow translators easy access to external MT services. Although they must be purchased separately from the provider of the MT tool, they are now progressively integrated with translation memories (TM) so translators are granted an instant pre-translated version of the given source text obtained from both TM and MT suggestions in one environment. Some freelance translators use such workstations on a daily basis and only revise the results, which makes their work quicker and thus more cost-effective. Other translators still refrain from such practices or are clearly instructed by the agencies they cooperate with that they are not allowed to use MT engines.

There are also situations when translators do not choose to use MT and TM suggestions combined but are confronted with such scenarios since "some translation agencies pre-translate their source files using a combination of TM and customized MT before sending them out to translators, who then become reviewers, or post-editors" (Teixeira, 2011: 108). The work of the translator who decides or is expected to mainly post-edit machine-generated translation differs significantly from the work of the translator who consciously decides to refrain from using CAT tools. The former operates on a segmented text, which implies that they focus on segments and check terminology and phraseology mostly, while the latter focuses broadly on the whole text, paying much more attention to the cohesion of the whole text. Working styles and thus general job characteristics of contemporary freelance translators can, therefore, differ to such an extent that little remains to compare. In fact, how the users of CAT tools work does not resemble the patterns associated with the work of non-users of CAT tools.

Although they belong to the same profession, the question arises as to whether there is still enough ground for comparison of users and non-users of CAT tools, especially when their work combines the automated machine translation output with active human post-editing. Irrespective of the great results offered by the use of machine translation, it reduces the translator's work to a machine-like process of decision-making, mostly based on a binary opposition since the translation decides whether the suggested segment is correct or not. Such a process of editing and revising leaves so little room for creative production that it can no longer be called translation. Helpful as post-edited machine translation can be, it truly dehumanises the process of translation and significantly diversifies the profile of the contemporary translator.

3.3 Technological Toolkit

Taking into consideration all of those differences in the translator profile and job characteristics of users and non-users of CAT tools (see sections 3.1–3.2), the technology-related aspects of translation make translator competence divergent and thus hardly operationalisable. Two different professionals can face utterly different problems in the process of translation. Additionally, the translation business is such a dynamic system that problems experienced currently may not be problems at all in the nearest future. In light of such a multifaceted and fast-changing profile of the translator, it can hardly be predicted what skills will be necessary for future translators. However, it needs to be emphasised here that – regardless of whether the present technological solutions will still be valid in the future – the basic set of instrumental skills and technical abilities related to information technology must at all costs be implemented in the translation classroom. This is also the stance of the EMT network (2017), that translation studies programmes must include substantial training in translation technology.

These are skills which serve the translator later in their professional career, so they should constitute a component of translation courses. Translation students need to be provided with a "technological toolkit," a set of skills necessary for successful interaction with translation technology. These are conceptual tools that help the translator make effective use of computer applications, software, corpus-based tools, web technologies, multimedia files, MT engines, and CAT tools as well as activities that are seemingly unrelated to translation, such as managing disc partitions for professional purposes or proper computer maintenance. In general, even such inconspicuous actions contribute to developing good working habits and thus ensure better functioning and safety of the translator's databank.

The technological toolkit is, therefore, a set of conceptual tools that make the translator "future proof" as it helps them to effectively function and handle technology. The principles of providing translation students with this toolkit include, but are not limited to, the following elements:

1. offering the opportunity to try out a number of technological tools used in the process of language service provision;
2. familiarising students with common problems occurring in TT interaction and potential ways to solve similar problems;
3. helping students develop skills of interacting with this type of technology successfully;
4. allowing for knowledge and experience acquisition in the context resembling their future context;
5. increasing awareness and readiness for future, self-directed TT interaction.

When translation students are provided with the technological toolkit, it is much easier for them to learn more and explore further technological developments on their own when they leave academia and enter the dynamic and ever-changing translation market. Thanks to that toolkit they will be more likely to self-regulate if need be and learn more about future technologies on their own so as to be able to find solutions to future problems that cannot be predicted now.

References

EMT Expert Group. (2009). *Competences for Professional Translators, Experts in Multilingual and Multimedia Communication*. Brussels: European Commission.

EMT Expert Group. (2017). *Competence Framework 2017* [Online]. Available at: https://ec.europa.eu/info/sites/info/files/emt_competence_fwk_2017_en_web. pdf (Accessed: 3 January 2020).

Enríquez Raído, Vanessa and Austermühl, Frank. (2003). Translation, Localization, and Technology: Current Developments. In: Gonzalez, Luis P. (ed.), *Speaking in Tongues: Language Across Contexts and Users*. València: Publicacions de la Universitat de València, pp. 225–250.

Gil, José R. B. and Pym, Anthony. (2006). Technology and Translation (a Pedagogical Overview). In: Pym, Anthony, Perekrestenko, Alexander and Starink, Bram (eds.), *Translation Technology and Its Teaching (With Much Mention of Localization)*. Intercultural Studies Group, Tarragona and Reus: Universitat Rovira i Virgili, pp. 5–19. ISBN: 978-84-611-1131-2

Hutchins, John. (1997). Translation Technology and the Translator. In: Greensmith, Catherine and Vandamme, Marilyn (eds.), *ITI Conference 11. Proceedings [of] International Conference, Exhibition & AGM*. London: Institute of Translation & Interpreting, pp. 113–120.

Kiraly, Don. (2000). *A Social Constructivist Approach to Translator Education. Empowerment from Theory to Practice*. Manchester: St Jerome.

PACTE Group. (2003). Building a Translation Competence Model. In: Alves, Fabio (ed.), *Triangulating Translation: Perspectives in Process Oriented Research*. Amsterdam: John Benjamins, pp. 43–65.

PACTE Group. (2005). Investigating Translation Competence: Conceptual and Methodological Issues. *Meta*, vol. 50(2), pp. 609–619.

Pym, Anthony. (2003). Redefining Translation Competence in an Electronic Age. In Defence of a Minimalist Approach. *META*, vol. XLVIII(4), pp. 481–497.

Pym, Anthony. (2011). What Technology Does to Translating. *Translation & Interpreting*, vol. 3(1), pp. 1–9.

Teixeira, Carlos. (2011). Knowledge of Provenance and Its Effects on Translation Performance. In: Sharp, Bernadette, Zock, Michael and Jakobsen, Arnt Lykke (eds.), *Human-Machine Interaction in Translation*. Frederiksberg: Samfundslitteratur, pp. 107–118.

Vieira, Lucas Nunes. (2018). Automation Anxiety and Translators. *Translation Studies*, https://doi.org/10.1080/14781700.2018.1543613

4 Technological Evolution in Translation

Overview of the Chapter

With technology changing the manner in which people work and communicate, the question of how translation technology is altering the translator's work systems is highly salient in contemporary translation studies. The effects of the application of CAT tools appear far-reaching and thus valid for translators and translation teachers. Provided that CAT technology is properly maintained and translators get accustomed to its characteristics, they can enjoy a number of advantages that directly influence their daily work. This chapter explores the key developments in CAT technology and their effects on the translator's work. It is shown that advancement in technology made it possible for CAT tools to support the translator in two major areas: proper translation and workflow management. The discussion of the advantages of CAT technology in the translation workspace and workflow (section 4.1) is followed by an analysis of the possible negative impact of CAT tools on the product and process of translation (section 4.2). Finally, the focus is laid on the cognitive and metacognitive aspects of TT interaction (section 4.3) with the discussion of the way translation technology affects the translator's psychological "self" (section 4.4) and the notion of anxiety related to the use of technology (section 4.5).

4.1 Key Developments in CAT Technology and Their Effects on the Translator's Work

Translation technology greatly affects translation with all its aspects (see Cronin, 2013; Doherty, 2016; Moorkens, 2017). The increasing popularity of translation technology and greater availability of Internet access resulted in a major technological shift in translation studies. As Pym (2011a: 1) observes, the use of translation technology alters "the very nature of the translator's cognitive activity, social relations, and professional standing." Translation technology contributes to a significant change in the way in which translators approach and manage their tasks and broadly defined workflow. What Chan (2004) calls a *technological turn* can be defined as a shift towards more automation in the translation process and translation project management.

The turn, or the shift, is a direct result of general advancements in information technology, which spur further changes in all the affected areas (e.g., in translation). The biggest and most profound change is the introduction of automation to the process of translation, be it project creation (e.g., in Memsource), TM match retrieval, or MT-based pre-translation, especially considering the fact that "approximately 40% of content translated takes advantage of previous translation work" (DePalma, 2012). Pym (2012) notes that MT-based pre-translation, while of considerable quality, is still used by LSPs as a rough first version of the translation, to be post-edited by a human translator. We see here that the shift, invoked by technology, is also reflected on the human translator level. The process of automation has to be directed and controlled by a supervisor who has the final word on what the target text will look like. Hence, the automation process can be successfully applied in order to prepare a rough translation, only to be polished (or post-edited) by the actual human translator. The main result of the turn, therefore, is the fact that the role of the human individual is slowly shifting from the translator to post-editor.

CAT technology has optimised the translation process to a large extent. First and foremost, it greatly enhanced the speed and efficiency of translation, which caused a lot of changes to the very process of translation. Furthermore, apart from helping translators work better and faster, new technological solutions enabled new ways of management, communication, and collaboration in the industry. CAT tools support the LSP-translator collaboration by enabling the LSP (or the translator when two individual translators collaborate and one takes the role of an LSP) to invite other professionals to work on the same document within the same tool, or allow multiple translators to work in real time on the same translation. What is more, many CAT tools store segment history which can be tracked and edited by other users. Finally, some CAT tools feature instant messengers, enabling LSPs and translators to communicate in real time.

With various services that support cross-language communication, CAT technology has been developing continuously, and its innovations have had a huge economic impact. The growth of CAT tools has been truly groundbreaking for translators who could "for the first time, easily create their own collections of stored translations for later reuse in their work, for sharing with their colleagues, and for both commercial and academic research purposes" (Doherty, 2016: 952). The development of translation technology can be divided into four periods (Chan, 2012), namely germination, growth, rapid growth, and the period of global development. The areas where CAT tools exert a strong influence on the process of translation are workspace and workflow.

According to Doherty (2016: 950), "the ongoing technological evolution in translation has yielded unprecedented gains in terms of increased translator productivity and consistency, greater global language coverage, and greater support for improving international communication and distribution." Contemporary CAT tools are powerful tools whose advantages can be discussed in reference to two areas of the translator's work: **proper translation** and **workflow management**. The primary role of a CAT tool is to assist a human translator in the process of translation, which falls under the first category mentioned here. The natural role of the tool is to help to translate within a special translation editor, **or a CAT-based translation workspace** (most tools use a similar two-column view of the translated document, with source segments on the left and target segments on the right, joined by TM/MT, TB, and preview panes to the right and bottom of the two). Such a layout, although usually fully adjustable, results from years of studies and feedback from translators and has become a standard of the translation industry. What differs is the individual UI of different tools, which is only natural and to be expected.

In order to start a translation, a translator has to enter the digital workspace of a CAT tool, create a new project, and import a source document. It is worth mentioning that CAT tools contain numerous filters that can be used in the case of certain types of documents (e.g., an HTML filter which filters out HTML tags from the source, allowing a translator to translate only the actual content of the document, without worrying about the proper placement of those tags). In most tools, filters are applied automatically based on the extension of the source file. However, translators can select filters manually if such a need arises. When the document is imported, a translator selects a translation memory (either one's own, the client's, or both) and termbase (again one's own, the client's, or both), and sets up an MT engine if available or required. During the translation process, the tool stores all new translations (or segments)[1] in a TM (automatically) and terms in a TB (manually). When the translator moves to a new segment, the programme checks all available resources for data that can be of use in the translation of this particular bit of the source document. The resources include matches from TM, TB, and MT, as well as quality assurance checks.

Depending on the tool, its settings, and available features, additional resources may be employed to assist the translator further (e.g., MTQE in Memsource). Once the translation is complete, it can be exported and delivered to a customer. It is the primary and most obvious advantage of CAT tools (and CAT-based translation workspace in particular) over regular translation. By having immediate access to all of the aforementioned resources, the translator can significantly speed up the process of translation, assuring at the same time translation and terminological coherence[2] throughout the entire project, or series of projects, for a given client. As a result, the translator can translate more content using CAT tools than they ever would without it. While this may be an obvious financial advantage, the real asset is the time saved, allowing the translator to accept bigger jobs with short deadlines and still manage to deliver them.

The second area where CAT technology proves particularly beneficial is **workflow** management. Most contemporary CAT tools allow freelancers to manage their jobs from within the tool to some extent, depending on the licence they own. **Basic workflow management** includes project management (adding new projects, setting deadlines, project analysis/quoting, adding/importing/exporting TMs, adding/importing/exporting TBs, translation, quality assessment, delivery, and project archiving). Those features allow the translator to store all projects in one structured repository of a CAT tool, with all related data (TMs, TBs) ready to be reused in the future. This functionality is sufficient for most freelance purposes and falls within the "translator tools" group proposed by Enríquez Raído and Austermühl (2003). The second type of management, which can be called **advanced workflow management**, involves additional features, aimed primarily at independent language service providers (ILSPs), translation agencies, and dedicated translation departments in companies. This set of features adds the possibility of outsourcing translation jobs (full or in parts), managing workflow steps (translation, revision, client/internal review), managing and distributing project resources (TMs, TBs, access to MT engines), and managing finances (clients, subcontractors). This group falls within the "localiser tools" category as proposed by Enríquez Raído and Austermühl (2003).

The list of features could be much longer depending on the tool since the advanced workflow is one of the areas where competition is most intense. New CAT tools (primarily SaaS) are offered free of charge in their "translator tool" version, while the "localiser" set of features are available for a fee. It has to be mentioned here that the advanced workflow management is not meant only for large translation companies. The term "independent language service providers" should be understood here also as individual freelancers who happen to be running their own translation businesses. When they run contracts for translation agencies/translation departments, they do not need any extra features.[3] These are needed in cases of independent jobs for end customers where ILSPs are responsible for the entire translation service (quote, translation, quality assurance, and delivery, to name the most basic steps). What is more, depending on the project, they may be required to outsource part of it due to, for example, a short deadline. Alternatively, the project may require additional proofreading by a native speaker – in which case the workflow step may be outsourced via licence sharing, assuring that all changes take place and are stored within the freelancer's CAT environment.

The majority of changes can be classified as improvements of the translator's work process. As can be seen from the data provided by CSA (DePalma, 2012), on average over 40% of the content for translation can take advantage of previous translation work. This implies a reduction in delivery times, as well as the cost of translation (40% of the job is proofreading/post-editing, which tends to cost less than a regular translation). As a result, more and more LSPs require translators to know and use at least one CAT tool in order to maximise their output and utilise the resources provided by the LSP (TM, TB, MT). What is more, the use of computer-assisted translation fuels the global market as well – now it is easier and faster than ever before to outsource translation jobs and collaborate in international teams, very much like in the IT industry.

4.2   Negative Impact of CAT Technology on the Process and Product

Despite numerous benefits of CAT tools, there are certain limitations of CAT systems as a whole that need to be acknowledged. Bundgaard (2017: 126) states that "while the CAT tool is generally expected to aid and support the translation process, it may also offer resistance and restrain the process in several ways." O'Brien et al. (2017: 145) observe that some freelancers still treat CAT tools with suspicion or disinterest since although they are "acknowledged to contribute to consistency and speed, they can constrain and otherwise negatively affect the translation process in various ways."

The disadvantages of the CAT tools can be divided into two categories: **system-related** and **user-related** issues. Before identifying and differentiating between them, it needs to be emphasised, however, that in many respects they affect one another to a certain degree. At the same time, the authors would like to stress that their focus lies solely with CAT tools as software and, therefore, they will not mention such issues as prolonged work or general problems related to computer-based translation, which are true both for regular and CAT-based translation.

System-related disadvantages of CAT tools are frequently tool-bound, although some generalisations can be made. For example, a thorough source document preparation is necessary prior to translation. While most CAT tools have robust filters for file import and segmentation, those do not always work properly, and segmentation errors do occur. If one considers the most frequent file formats used to store documents – DOC/X and

PDF – one will notice segmentation differences not only between the two formats but also between different tools. While virtually all CAT tools can import PDF files (provided they contain actual text, not images of text), the segmentation can be way off, or "broken," depending on the way in which the PDF was prepared in the first place. The abundance of computer text editing software that can save PDF files makes it impossible to predict when a given document will "work" with CAT tools and when it will not. When it "works," the programme will import the file and break the text into segments according to its internal rules, mostly into single sentences. When it does not "work," for example when the PDF text breaks at the end of each line with a hard return (or paragraph ending marker), the segmentation algorithm in CAT tools is prone to produce segmentation errors. For example, one of the default segmentation rules is that a segment ends at the end of a paragraph. With each line broken with a paragraph ending information (hard return), the system breaks sentences into bits which have to be joined manually from within the translation editor in CAT tool. Obviously enough, software developers are aware of the problem, and part of the CAT tool "refinement" process is devoted to such problems – a tool analyses entire blocks of text, tries to determine the actual shape of sentences, and joins them automatically. As highly advanced as CAT tools are, they are still only computer programmes and do not share human abilities to sort and solve such problems in all contexts. As a result, in order to avoid such problems, thorough preparation of the source document is necessary (it may be compared to pre-editing in MT).

Another system-related issue involves tool (in)compatibility. While it is possible to move TMs and TBs between different tools (to some extent and using only open exchange formats like TMX, TBX, or XLSX), it is virtually impossible to collaborate on the same project using different tools. The problem lies in content distribution and the different system architecture of different tools. When a CAT project is shared between multiple vendors (or subcontractors), two methods can be applied.

The first one (offline) requires a project manager to divide a project into jobs, save those jobs as translation packages,[4] and send them to respective vendors. The problem here is that not all tools accept packages created in other tools, and even if they do, some features may be disabled, or worse, work in the wrong way, simply due to differences in the internal architecture of CAT systems. For that reason, it is safer to work only with those translators who use exactly the same tool as the one used to create and divide the project.

The second one (online) requires LSPs to use a CAT tool that can handle cloud, or server, projects (like memoQ server or Memsource). In this case, a project is divided online and shared with individual vendors as SaaS, not as translation packages. Such a solution, more and more popular, negates the problem of incompatibility because the translators have to use the same tool as the project manager who created the project in the first place. Depending on the tool, translators either log in to the cloud of the LSP and translate the content shared there or use their own tool to access a server project. Either way, the incompatibility problem is recognised and resolved at the project manager's level.

One more purely system-related disadvantage of CAT tools is the system requirements (operating system [OS] in particular). While research on CAT tools was, and is, by no means centralised and one could expect CAT software to be developed on any widely available OS, a vast majority of CAT tools are bound to MS Windows. Most probably, this is related to the OS distribution on desktop computers. According to StatCounter Global-Stats, a web analytics service which analyses online traffic, Windows-based desktop computers take first place with 78.43% of the market, with OS X (13.53%) and Linux (1.6 %)[5] coming in second and third, respectively. Considering the cost involved in developing specialised software like CAT tools, other-than-Windows computer platforms might not have been worth the time and money invested into developing separate OS versions; it needs to be taken into consideration that developing software for a given platform requires not only the tool but constant supervision, development, and future updates. With the majority of the CAT market taken by Windows-bound CAT tools like SDL Trados or memoQ, users of non-Windows systems had limited access to CAT tools also because of the compatibility issues mentioned earlier. However, it has to be noted that the trend is shifting as more and more CAT tools are created as (or move to) SaaS and cloud computing systems. It means that they are (re)developed to work in an Internet browser and become OS independent (e.g., Memsource).

On the other hand, user-related problems can (in some respects) result from a subconscious acceptance of computer-suggested translation solutions by the human translator. The problem is quite complex and, again, grounded on the mechanics of CAT tools. The first problem, as suggested for example, by Ehrensberger-Dow and Massey (2014: 6), is related to text segmentation and its influence on the translator's choices in this respect:

An interesting case study of the constraining influence of tools is provided by a simple comparison of target texts produced with and without TM. In the lab, with no TM available, professionals translated into German an English source text that had three long sentences. . . . [T]he shortest sentence was always translated as a single sentence but the longest one as two sentences. By contrast, when the same professionals translated source-text sentences of comparable length using TM in the workplace, these were rendered as single sentences 50% of the time. The sentence segmentation typical of most TM system settings (cf. LeBlanc, 2013) may unintentionally **constrain creativity and the freedom to move away from source-text syntactic patterns.**[6]

Segmentation may affect the style of translation as well. While, in theory, technical texts will suffer less since they contain few metaphors or figures of speech, general and humanities texts may lack in this respect. It is a common case, therefore, that translators proofread their translations for style outside the segment-to-segment environment of CAT tools and reintroduce any resulting changes into the CAT tool afterwards in order to update translation memory.

A related problem is connected to matches offered by translation memories provided by clients. While the translator can trust, to an extent, their own TM (containing their own translations), the same should not be said about TMs obtained from external sources. Kornacki (2018: 14) mentions that "Bowker (2005) and Doherty (2016) suggest that many translators have adopted the so-called 'blind faith' in the previously used human translation, stored in translation memories. As a result, they assume (often erroneously) that the data are of high quality and does not require as close evaluation as in the case of translation from scratch." The problem with such an assumption is that translators do not know whom the author of a given translation is while having to check the match against the context of a given document and decide whether to use it or not (if the translation is faulty or unacceptable altogether). Doherty (2016: 954) suggests that this tendency can be "compounded by the reduced remuneration for using TMs," which is related to why the TM was provided in the first place.

Nevertheless, taking into consideration the characteristics of CAT technology discussed in previous sections, with all its advantages and disadvantages, it must be concluded that CAT tools are a great help in the translation business.

4.3   Cognitive Aspects of TT Interaction

From a cognitive perspective, the mental processes of translation and the translator's metacognitive skills are also affected by the technology used in the process of translation. As Mossop (2006: 789) observes, "a closer look at workplaces might reveal that new work procedures accompanying the changes in translation as a business have brought about some changes in the mental process of translation production." He discusses the issues of greater speed, more chunking of text, more division of work, and less time for quality control, which is accompanied by changes in the mental process of translation (ibid.). The result of the aforementioned changes is what Mossop (2006: 790) describes as a situation when "very often no one has an overview of the text as a semantic whole," and the phenomenon of collage translation when "composing a translation on a blank screen is replaced by revision of old TL material from a variety of sources to make it match the source text, together with varying amounts of effort to smooth the joins between the various parts of the resulting collage." What Mossop (ibid.: 793) means is that there is a situation when "the old TL material may be acquired in automated fashion using translation memory software, but this is not necessary to create a collage; translators can also manually cut and paste existing TL material into the translation they are creating" (ibid.: 793).

Such a process of translation differs significantly from what it used to be before the advent of CAT technology. It was as early as 2011 that Anthony Pym (2011b: 421) envisaged the change in the nature of translation services "with many of today's translators becoming tomorrow's technical writers (pre-editors) or reviewers of machine translations (post-editors)." Pym (2011a: 1) discusses the impact of technology on the translator's perception and claims that it affects the translator's memory. He argues that

> technologies first affect memory capacity in such a way that the paradigmatic is imposed more frequently on the syntagmatic. It follows that the translating activity is enhanced in its generative moment, yet potentially retarded in the moment of selection, where the values of intuition and text flow become difficult to recuperate.

Some of the features and functionalities of CAT tools, such as segmentation, vocabulary auto-insertion, and text prediction reduce the process of creation to mere decision-making.

Changes that occur in the translation workflow clearly influence the cognitive processes that underlie translation and also metacognitive skills of the translator, as will be discussed in the following section.

4.4   Impact of CAT Technology and TT Interaction on Translator's Metacognition

Although it must be acknowledged and appreciated that the productivity of the translator has considerably grown since the advent of CAT tools, their popularity can cause certain worries not only when it comes to physical but also psycho-physical aspects of the translator's profession. As PACTE (2003: 58) states, translation competence "is made up of five subcompetencies (bilingual, extra-linguistic, knowledge about translation, instrumental and strategic) and it activates a series of psycho-physiological mechanisms"

(2003: 58). Those psycho-physiological components are described as follows:

> Different types of cognitive and attitudinal components and psycho-motor mechanisms. They include: (1) cognitive components such as memory, perception, attention and emotion; (2) attitudinal aspects such as intellectual curiosity, perseverance, rigour, critical spirit, knowledge of and confidence in one's own abilities, the ability to measure one's own abilities, motivation, etc.; (3) abilities such as creativity, logical reasoning, analysis and synthesis, etc.
>
> (ibid.)

Psychological aspects of translator competence are also included in the description of what the aforementioned model calls strategic competence, which plays a central role in the translation process as

> its functions are: to plan the process and carry out the translation project (selecting the most appropriate method), to evaluate the process and the partial results obtained in relation to the final purpose, to activate the different subcompetences and compensate for any shortcomings and to identify translation problems and apply procedures to solve them.
>
> (PACTE, 2003: 58)

Göpferich (2009: 18) also discusses the psycho-physical disposition of the translator and adds that strategic competence involves "the competence to develop an adequate macro-strategy and to employ it consistently."

All of the mental processes referred to as strategic behaviour "map onto metacognition" (Muñoz Martín, 2014: 26). Metacognition of the translator "(also self-regulation, executive control, executive processes) . . . involves active control over the component cognitive processes involved in translation" Shreve (2006: 39). Metacognition is often described as involving both *knowledge* and *regulation* of mental processes. Metacognitive knowledge is what people know about themselves, about how they use their minds, and about how tasks are carried out. Metacognitive regulation comprises the set of goal-directed processes individuals engage in to coordinate and steer their mental activities. In turn, regulation subdivides into *monitoring* and *control* (ibid.: 26).

Bandura (1994: 72) defines self-regulation as the "exercise of influence over one's own motivation, thought processes, emotional states and patterns of behaviour". Self-regulated translators set their goals cautiously, choose the most appropriate strategies to achieve them, but also organise their work effectively and reflect on the process (Pietrzak, 2018: 822).

Those metacognitive skills of the translator can be affected by CAT technology since the more complex the translator-technology (TT) interaction becomes, the more changes occur in the translation workflow and thus the translator's schemata of work. Years of working with CAT tools affect their cognitive development and influence metacognitive aspects that make up the translator's metacognitive knowledge and metacognitive regulation, both in positive and negative ways. The three core areas of metacognition that will be examined here are **self-development, self-reliance**, and **self-efficacy**.

Intrinsic motivations and drives of the translator change during TT interaction. In translation, those schemata are patterns of thoughts and behaviours that organise translator competence and the perception of the translation task. In Piagetian (1951) constructivist epistemology, the schemata that people construct are based on perceptions and interactions that they experience. TT interaction causes the translator's environment to change rapidly and thus requires translators to organise new metacognitive perceptions into schemata. The question arises as to what influence those changes exert on the translator's **self-development**. In TT interaction, new regularities occur and provoke "sequences of behaviours adapted to these regularities" (Georgeon and Ritter, 2012: 73). In this process of adaptation, the translator's metacognitive behaviours change. This is solving translation problems and searching for best solutions that drive learning and development. In the past, when translators used to search for information, they very often would conduct long research before choosing one translation solution over the other, so the whole process of analysing the possible options and decision-making contributed to self-learning and gaining more background knowledge in the researched field. Despite the positive effect and all its advantages, one of the potential adverse effects of CAT technology on the translator's self-concept is the issue of little self-development.

As far as **self-reliance** is concerned, in the case of young or inexperienced translators, the problems of overreliance on CAT technology cannot be disregarded. Translators who are used to working with the help of translation technology are likely to appreciate the assistance to such an extent that they value the suggested translation solutions too much. Young and inexperienced translators often fail to realise that MT suggestions happen to be inaccurate, and they simply accept them without much concern about translation quality and the final outcome of their work. There seems to be a growing problem with excessive trust in machine translation and relying heavily on the suggestions offered by technological solutions (cf. Kornacki, 2018; Bowker, 2005; Doherty, 2016).

The third area where the adverse effect of the use of CAT tools can be observed is the translator's self-influence or, more precisely, one of the mechanisms behind it called **self-efficacy** (i.e., "the belief in one's personal efficacy" (Bandura, 2009: 179)). As Bandura (1992: 122) defines it, self-efficacy is the personal judgement of "how well one can execute courses of action required to deal with prospective situations." According to Muñoz Martín (2014: 18), self-efficacy is one of the three components (together with self-awareness and situation awareness) of the self-concept of the translator. He defines the self-concept as one of the five dimensions of "a minimal, situated concept of general translation expertise" together with knowledge, adaptive psycho-physiological traits, problem-solving skills, and regulatory skills. As Kiraly (1995: 100) defines it, the translator's self-concept is

> a sense of purpose of the translation, an awareness of the information requirements of the translation task, a self-evaluation of the capability to fulfil the task, and a related capacity to monitor and evaluate translation products for adequacy and appropriateness.

What can be seen as a factor that adversely affects the translator's self-concept and the broadly defined translator's psychological "self" (see Haro-Soler and Kiraly, 2019) is the helplessness in the face of technology failure or just a temporary lack of CAT technology. The use of translation technology affects the translator's self-efficacy through its effects on not only motivation processes but also performance efficiency. Translators who are accustomed to working with the assistance of CAT tools are likely to get discouraged when faced with a long source text to be translated in a traditional way. They may feel unable to effectively cope with problematic issues that used to be solved by technology.

Bandura (1994: 74) observes that "the stronger the perceived self-efficacy, the higher the goal challenges people set for themselves, and the firmer is their commitment to them." High self-efficacy helps people develop effective task strategies (Latham et al., 1994; Wood and Bandura, 1989). Interestingly, Locke and Latham (2002: 707) note that "if the path to the goal is not a matter of using automatized skills, people draw from a repertoire of skills that they have used previously in related contexts, and they apply them to the present situation." In the translation industry, translators use their skills from before technological advancements and apply them when using translation technology. On the other hand, translators who work solely with CAT tools and do not have automatised skills of translating with pen and paper are not likely to adapt to new working conditions as they lack the repertoire of those essential skills.

Translators who use CAT tools extensively in their daily work are likely to feel less readiness to cope with a problem without computer assistance.

The dependence on CAT tools can negatively affect not only the translator's ability to translate but also the perception of their own ability to translate without the aid of CAT tools and thus their work performance without the actual usage of technology. The correlation between the use of translation technology and the translator's metacognitive skills has received little coverage in translation studies so far, but it would be an interesting area for further research. The question that arises and has yet to be answered is whether the contemporary translator would still be able to translate with mere pen and paper if the need arose.

4.5   Technology-Related Anxiety in Freelance Translation

Moving from the negative aspects that translation technology can have for the translator's self-concept in the long run, the following section focuses on another problematic issue related to CAT tools, namely the issue of anxiety. Since freelance translators often experience anxiety at many different points of their professional life, it will now be analysed with a particular interest in technology-related anxiety. As Vieira (2018) observes, "advances in machine translation (MT) technology and the reverberations of the 2008 financial crisis have led to perceptions of translation as a profession under pressure from automation, falling prices and globalized competition." The following section discusses the issue of anxiety in the profession of a freelance translator, as it can take various forms and have many origins.

4.5.1   Career Anxiety

In the light of the rapid development of machine translation and artificial intelligence, translators are concerned about their own career. To some extent, their professional life depends on technological progress, which constantly brings innovation to the translation business. As it can be observed in the results of the study discussed in section 6 of the present book, the participants who have been asked to air their views on MT-assisted translation expressed a lot of concerns related to their own career. It is hard to predict the changes or estimate the probability that a given CAT tool will outperform another technological tool.

Such unpredictability can cause anxiety related not only to worries about their own career but also about the future of the very profession. "The translator is becoming more and more dependent on information technology and, if the translator does not adapt to change, he or she may become uncompetitive" (Samuelsson-Brown, 1996: 280). When they begin their career as young translators, translators may experience anxiety about their future career.

Nevertheless, despite various fears and worries, "technology tends to replace specific tasks rather than entire occupations" (Autor, 2015: 26), especially if these occupations require competence that is not easily definable and, thus, programmable. It has been observed by Vieira (2018) that only certain aspects have been automated by CAT tools. While these tools also include MT output as a feature that can be used in the translation process, as the name suggests, they assist rather than replace human translators. Users of these tools would still translate from scratch where required as well as edit and interact with suggestions from MT systems and/or translation memories, among other tasks.

In the process of computer-assisted translation, only certain tasks can be automated, and the preliminary condition is that the tasks are recurrent in nature. Although machine translation technology has recently become more and more widespread amongst both LSPs and freelancers, there is still very strong anxiety about using MT resources. The first and foremost problem most translators have with machine translation is that the source of the suggestion of the translation is not always known and, therefore, its accuracy in a given context cannot be determined. Of course, the issue would be irrelevant if the translator knew exactly how to translate a given string of text (MT match being there only to support his/her choice of words), but that is not always the case, especially considering the volume of text freelancers have to process daily. The second issue at hand is confidentiality. We live in a global society which shares a lot of data, whether we want it to or not. While this may cause potential problems in private life, unrestricted (or uncontrolled) data sharing is anathema in professional life. Translators frequently deal with texts which require separate confidentiality clauses to be signed between the client and the translators and, therefore, any potential data security issues have to be properly addressed. Machine translation can be considered a security threat. The problem is that freelancers translate texts – they do not conduct data security audits. We are recommended to use state-of-the-art computer software to aid us in the translation process, but we do not know if, and how much, data such tools learn from us. It is yet another example of the technological anxiety mentioned before – on the one hand, translators would like to use resources that may potentially ease and speed up their work, and on the other, they are unsure if they accidentally violate any confidentiality agreements by which they may be bound (see, for example, Zaretskaya et al., 2015: 82).

Interestingly, Vieira (2018) predicts another potential threat, namely the situation in which there is an increased interest in working in the translation industry caused by higher unemployment in other professions that are more threatened by globalisation and technological innovation. The profession of the translator is, therefore, not directly threatened by technology but may be affected by general working conditions and the market situation.

Translators worry about the potential decrease in their compensation because of the progress in automation. Vieira (2018) discusses the problem of this automation anxiety among translators and is fairly optimistic when it comes to translators' pay. Vieira (2018) states that, although there has been a fall in translation rates reported by Doherty (2016: 949), there are numerous studies that show a "mixed picture rather than a pronounced downward trend," which suggests that

> either not all translators are experiencing falling rates, or that for some translators technology's downward effect on unit rates can be compensated by an increase in volume, as some of the results above correspond to overall pay rather than rates per word.

4.5.2   *Cognitive Friction*

The translator's interaction with technology can be as rewarding as it can be frustrating. It has already been acknowledged that translator-computer interaction (TCI) can cause irritation to the users (O'Brien, 2012), which Ehrensberger-Dow and O'Brien (2015: 103) call cognitive friction (i.e., the irritation that occurs when the state of "flow" is disturbed by organisational, task, or technological issues) and is "assumed to detract from the efficiency of the translation process, with potentially negative consequences on translator performance and satisfaction."

The extent of translator-technology (TT) interaction differs significantly among freelance translators (see section 2.2). The success of TT interaction can be highly dependent on the translator's IT skills but also other factors that are outside the translator's control. If the translator comes across a malfunction, it interrupts their work and forces them to deal with the problem with either hardware or software on their own or have it addressed by a technician. On the other hand, the more complex the translator-computer interaction gets, the greater the tendency for even most complex processes to get simplified with time and technological progress. The features that seem discouraging for translators now may belong to the past sooner than we expect.

The authors would like to make a distinction between two types of anxiety related to CAT tools. The discomfort called cognitive friction is usually caused by random situations in the process of translation. As O'Brien et al. (2017: 147) put it, cognitive friction occurs when an extraneous cognitive load caused by "unhelpful or distracting CAT tool features" is combined with the "intrinsic load of the translation task itself." Another type of anxiety in translation is what the authors call technological anxiety.

4.5.3 Technological Anxiety

In contrast to cognitive friction, which occurs and thus hinders the process of translation, technological anxiety actually prevents the process of translation from happening. This type of anxiety is the fear of computer assistance based on the assumption that a potential problem occurs in the process of translation and causes trouble that would be too difficult to solve. At the same time, it has to be stated that the concept is not the same as the notion of computer anxiety, as discussed by Brosnan (1998), Rosen et al. (1993), or Gilbert et al. (2003), for example. The authors understand the concept as one relating more to translation technology (see chapter 2) as such, rather than to CAT technology. In translation, this type of anxiety is usually caused by a lack of familiarity with certain technological tools available on the market.

Translators who experience this type of anxiety do not believe that they are able to adequately deal with computer-related problems. It is a fear of the inability to accept new technological challenges, discover the means to face them, and successfully incorporate learned skills in the future. At the same time, it is the direct opposite of technological flexibility, another psychological property, which was signalled in section 1.2. It is fear not of technology as such but rather of one's own ability to master it and fear of failure in this respect. Many people suffer from technological anxiety; hence not everyone can be successful in a profession that requires mastering some aspects of computer technology. Add to that the fact that the market becomes even more globalised day by day, and we can see the dire need for a pro-technological approach to the profession of a translator, which will be discussed later in the course of the book.

In fact, both aspects of anxiety mentioned by the authors can be regarded as mild instances of technophobia. According to Rosen and Maguire (1990: 276), technophobia is

> anxiety about current or future interactions with computers or computer-related technology; negative global attitudes about computers, their operation or their societal impact; and/or specific negative cognitions or self-critical internal dialogues during actual computer interactions or when contemplating future interaction.

Depending on the severity of the anxiety, Rosen et al. (1993) categorise computer users as "uncomfortable users," "cognitive computerphobes," and the "anxious computerphobes." Unless the use of computers is forced on them, translators fall into the first group. What is particularly interesting, however, is the fact that researchers have shown (e.g., Brosnan, 1998) that there is a "relationship between computer anxiety and demographic variables such as age, gender and academic qualifications" (Gilbert et al., 2003: 254). Apparently, females are more prone to computer anxiety than males (Igbaria and Chakrabarti, 1990; Okebukola and Woda, 1993; Farina et al., 1991; Brosnan and Davidson, 1996; as cited in Gilbert et al., 2003). However, Brosnan (1998) suggested that women are more likely to use computers when it has a direct use in their lives, which is reflected in the translation industry where approximately three in four translators are female (Pym, 2012).

The profession of a translator is especially susceptible to technological anxiety. Freelancers often work under pressure of time and quality, the market becomes more and more competitive, and technology ceases to be an option – it has become a requirement. It has to be emphasised that not all translators use technology to the same extent (see section 2.2). Some of them are content to rely on basic tools like word processors to do their job, so their risk of technological anxiety is much smaller than in those who have to use CAT tools and MT engines daily, for instance. Both groups of translators have taken part in the study presented in chapters 5 and 6.

Notes

1. Please refer to Kornacki (2018: 107) for terminology disambiguation.
2. Translation coherence in this respect results from a conscious choice of a translator to retain the same translation of a given, repetitive segment throughout the entire job/series of jobs. While this may be an asset, sometimes it results in errors due to reusing a given translation in a bad context.
3. Actually, frequently they do not need their own CAT tool licence as many LSPs share licences with their contractors (e.g., project managers in memoQ can share licences from their licence pools over CAL (Concurrent Access Licensing) or ELM (Enterprise License Management), depending on their server configuration). Similarly, project managers in Memsource can do the same, the number of available licences depending on their subscription plan. Depending on a tool, a contractor licence can be shared indefinitely, for a period of time, or it can be bound to a given translation job (expiring after the job is completed). Licence sharing allows project managers to make sure the translators use the same CAT tool for translation, assuring 100% compatibility between the project's back- and front-end.
4. In theory, the same can be achieved by sending each translator a DOCX file with source content, TMX file with TM, and TBX file with TB. While the authors acknowledge that incidentally such may be case, it is against the idea behind CAT tools, which are designed to facilitate work both for a translator and project manager/LSP. Distribution of packages facilitates the process through simplification. When a translation package is returned, LSP imports it into the larger body of a project, updating the translation, TM, and TB in one go. Considering the amount of content translated daily, content packaging is much faster.
5. Desktop computers. Data as of July 2019. Please visit http://gs.statcounter.com/os-market-share/desktop/worldwide/ for current data.
6. Bold by the authors.

References

Autor, David H. (2015). Why Are There Still so Many Jobs? The History and Future of Workplace Automation. *Journal of Economic Perspectives*, vol. 29(3), pp. 3–30.

Bandura, Albert. (1992). Self-efficacy Mechanism in Human Agency. *American Psychologist*, vol. 37, pp. 122–147. https://doi.org/10.1037/0003-066X.37.2.122

Bandura, Albert. (1994). Self-efficacy. In: Ramachaudran, V. S. (ed.), *Encyclopedia of Human Behavior*. Vol. 4. New York: Academic Press, pp. 71–81. (Reprinted in Friedman, H. [ed.], *Encyclopedia of Mental Health*. San Diego: Academic Press, 1998).

Bandura, Albert. (2009). Cultivate Self-efficacy for Personal and Organizational Effectiveness. In: Locke, E. A. (ed.), *Handbook of Principles of Organization Behavior*, 2nd ed. New York: Wiley, pp. 179–200.

Bowker, Lynne. (2005). Productivity vs Quality? A Pilot Study on the Impact of Translation Memory Systems. *Localisation Focus*, vol. 4(1), pp. 13–20.

Brosnan, Mark. (1998). *Technophobia, The Psychological Impact of Information Technology*. New York, NY: Routledge.

Brosnan, Mark and Davidson, Marylin J. (1996). Psychological Gender Issues in Computing. *Journal of Gender, Work and Organization*, vol. 3(1), pp. 13–25.

Bundgaard, Kristine. (2017). Translator Attitudes Towards Translator-Computer Interaction – Findings from a Workplace Study. *HERMES-Journal of Language and Communication in Business*, pp. 125–144.

Chan, Sin-Wei. (2004). *A Dictionary of Translation Technology*. Hong Kong: The Chinese University Press.

Chan, Sin-Wei. (2012). *Translation Technology: Past, Present and Future*. Paper presented at the 2012 LTTC International Conference: The Making of a Translator, Taipei.

Cronin, Michael. (2013). *Translation in the Digital Age*. London and New York: Routledge.

DePalma, Donald A. (2012). *Translation Future Shock*, pp. 16–18. [Private online access]. (Accessed: 9 July 2019).

Doherty, Stephen. (2016). The Impact of Translation Technologies on the Process and Product of Translation. *International Journal of Communication*, vol. 10, pp. 947–969.

Ehrensberger-Dow, Maureen and Massey, Gary. (2014). *Constraints on Creativity: The Case of CAT Tools* [Online]. Available at: www.researchgate.net/publication/278676021_Constraints_on_creativity_The_case_of_CAT_tools (Accessed: 24 July 2019).

Ehrensberger-Dow, Maureen and O'Brien, Sharon. (2015). Ergonomics of the Translation Workplace: Potential for Cognitive Friction. *Translation Spaces*, vol. 4(1), pp. 98–118.

Enríquez Raído, Vanessa and Austermühl, Frank. (2003). Translation, Localization, and Technology: Current Developments. In: Gonzalez, Luis P. (ed.), *Speaking in Tongues: Language Across Contexts and Users*. València: Publicacions de la Universitat de València, pp. 225–250.

Farina, Francisca, Arce, Ramon, Sobral, Jorge and Carames, Rosa. (1991). Predictors of Anxiety Towards Computers. *Computers in Human Behaviour*, vol. 7(4), pp. 263–267.

Georgeon, Olivier and Ritter, Frank E. (2012). An Intrinsically-Motivated Schema Mechanism to Model and Simulate Emergent Cognition. *Cognitive Systems Research*, vol. 15–16, pp. 73–92.

Gilbert, David, Lee-Kelley, Liz and Barton, Maya. (2003). Technophobia, Gender Influences and Consumer Decision-Making for Technology-Related Products. *European Journal of Innovation Management*, vol. 6(4), pp. 253–263.

Göpferich, Susanne. (2009). Towards a Model of Translation Competence and Its Acquisition: The Longitudinal Study Transcomp. In: Göpferich, Susanne, Jakobsen, Arne L. and Mees, Ingrid M. (eds.), *Behind the Mind: Methods, Models and Results in Translation Process Research*. Copenhagen: Samfundslitteratur Press, pp. 11–37.

Haro-Soler, Maria and Kiraly, Don. (2019). Exploring Self-efficacy Beliefs in Symbiotic Collaboration with Students: an Action Research Project. *The Interpreter and Translator Trainer*, vol. 13(3), pp. 255–270.

Igbaria, Magid and Chakrabarti, Alogk. (1990). Computer Anxiety and Attitudes Towards Microcomputer Use. *Behaviour & Information Technology*, vol. 9(3), pp. 229–241.

Kiraly, Don. (1995). *Pathways to Translation: Pedagogy and Process*. Kent: Kent State University Press.

Kornacki, Michał. (2018). *Computer-assisted Translation (CAT) Tools in the Translator Training Process*. Berlin: Peter Lang.

Latham, Gary P., Winters, Dawn C. and Locke, Edwin A. (1994). Cognitive and Motivational Effects of Participation: A Mediator Study. *Journal of Organizational Behavior*, vol. 15, pp. 49–63. https://doi.org/10.1002/job.4030150106

LeBlanc, Matthieu. (2013). Translators on Translation Memory (TM). Results of an Ethnographic Study in Three Translation Services and Agencies. *The International Journal for Translation & Interpreting Research*, vol. 5(2), pp. 1–13.

Locke, Edwin A. and Latham, Gary P. (2002). Building a Practically Useful Theory of Goal Setting and Task Motivation. *American Psychologist*, vol. 57(9), pp. 705–717.

Moorkens, Joss. (2017). Under Pressure: Translation in Times of Austerity. *Perspectives Studies in Translatology*, vol. 25(3), pp. 464–477.

Mossop, Brian. (2006). Has Computerization Changed Translation? *META*, vol. 51(4), pp. 1–9. https://doi.org/10.7202/014342ar

Muñoz Martín, Ricardo. (2014). Situating Translation Expertise: A Review with a Sketch of a Construct. In: Schwieter, John and Ferreira, Aline (eds.), *The Development of Translation Competence: Theories and Methodologies from Psycholinguistics and Cognitive Science*. Cambridge: Cambridge Scholars Publishing, pp. 2–54.

O'Brien, Sharon. (2012). Translation as Human-Computer Interaction. *Translation Spaces*, vol. 1(1), pp. 101–122.

O'Brien, Sharon, Ehrensberger-Dow, Maureen, Hasler, Marcel and Connolly, Megan. (2017). Irritating CAT Tool Features that Matter to Translators. *HERMES-Journal of Language and Communication in Business*, vol. 56, pp. 145–162.

Okebukola, Peter and Woda, Augustinus. (1993). The Gender Factor in Computer Anxiety and Interest Among Some Australian High School Students. *Educational Research*, vol. 35(2), pp. 181–189.

PACTE Group. (2003). Building a Translation Competence Model. In: Alves, Fabio (ed.), *Triangulating Translation: Perspectives in Process Oriented Research*. Amsterdam: John Benjamins, pp. 43–65.

Piaget, Jean. (1951). *The Psychology of Intelligence*. London: Routledge and Kegan Paul.

Pietrzak, Paulina. (2018). The Effects of Students' Self-regulation on Translation Quality. *Babel: International Journal of Translation*, vol. 64(5/6), pp. 819–839.

Pym, Anthony. (2011a). What Technology Does to Translating. *Translation & Interpreting*, vol. 3(1), pp. 1–9.

Pym, Anthony. (2011b). Website Localization. In: Malmkjaer, Kirsten and Windle, Kevin (eds.), *The Oxford Handbook for Translation Studies*. Oxford: Oxford University Press, pp. 410–424.

Pym, Anthony. (2012). Translation Skill-Sets in a Machine-Translation Age. *Meta*, vol. 58(3), pp. 487–503. https://doi.org/10.7202/1025047ar

Rosen, Larry D. and Maguire, Phyllisann. (1990). *Myths and Realities of Computerphobia: a Meta-analysis. Anxiety Research*, vol. 3, pp. 175–191.

Rosen, Larry D., Sears, Deborah C. and Weil, Michelle M. (1993). Treating Technophobia: A Longitudinal Evaluation of the Computerphobia Reduction Program. *Computers in Human Behaviour*, vol. 9, pp. 27–50.

Samuelsson-Brown, Geoffrey. (1996). New Technology for Translators. In: Owens, Rachel (ed.), *The Translator's Handbook*. London: Aslib, pp. 279–293.

Shreve, Gregory M. (2006). The Deliberate Practice: Translation and Expertise. *Journal of Translation Studies*, vol. 9(1), pp. 27–42.

Vieira, Lucas Nunes. (2018). Automation Anxiety and Translators. *Translation Studies*, https://doi.org/10.1080/14781700.2018.1543613

Wood, Robert and Bandura, Albert. (1989). Impact of Conceptions of Ability on Self-regulatory Mechanisms and Complex Decision Making. *Journal of Personality and Social Psychology*, vol. 56(3), pp. 407–415. https://doi.org/10.1037/0022-3514.56.3.407

Zaretskaya, Anna, Corpas Pastor, Gloria and Seghiri, Miriam. (2015). Integration of Machine Translation in CAT Tools: State of the Art, Evaluation and User Attitudes. *SKASE Journal for Translation and Interpretation*, vol. 8(1), pp. 76–88.

5 Current Trends in the Use of CAT Tools in Freelance Translation

Overview of the Chapter

To provide more insight regarding the use of CAT tools in freelance translation, this chapter discusses the results of a research study conducted on professional translators who are either users or non-users of CAT technology. The study was designed to explore the attitudes and preferences of freelance translators working with various language pairs whose native language is Polish. Section 5.1 outlines the methodology, aims, procedures applied, tools used for data collection and analysis, as well as the limitations of the study. The main assumption underlying the study is that, despite all the benefits of computer-assisted translation, the translation market remains divided into users and non-users of CAT tools. Section 5.2 discusses the approach of freelance translators to academia and this kind of study.

5.1 The Methodology Behind the Study on CAT Users and Non-Users

The research was based on a survey directed to professional translators in Poland. The information regarding the questionnaire was published on the closed Facebook group "Tłumacze," one of the meeting grounds for professional translators in Poland. As of 1 March 2019, the group listed 4,579 members. Additionally, it was sent over e-mail to those sworn translators in Poland (all languages), who have provided their contact e-mail on the list of sworn translators (www.ms.gov.pl/pl/lista-tlumaczy-przysieglych/), published by the Ministry of Justice of Poland, 2,914 sworn translators in total. The notification was made in Polish and included a short explanation regarding what the survey is about, together with a link to a website where the first question of the survey ("Do you use CAT tools on a daily basis?") was published. The answer, either Yes or No, redirected respondents to the respective Google Form with a sub-questionnaire for CAT users (Yes) or

CAT non-users (No). In total, the authors of the survey collected responses from 141 professional translators working in the Polish language.

5.1.1 Aim of the Study

The study aims to show the existing tendencies and mechanisms in the use of CAT tools and explore the reasons for the apparent reluctance towards those tools in the freelance translation market. The main research question that guided the exploratory study on freelance translators was to determine their attitudes and preferences regarding the use of CAT technology in general, and CAT tools in particular. The main assumption underlying the study is that, despite all the benefits of computer-assisted translation, the translation market remains divided into users and non-users of CAT tools.

5.1.2 Tools for Data Collection and Analysis

The study was conducted using the CAWI (Computer-Assisted Web Interview) technique based on a questionnaire. The survey was available to the respondents during the period between January and February 2019. It should be noted that the population of freelance translators is difficult to determine numerically. What is more, there is no sampling frame for this population. This study attempted to identify the tested subjects using two paths:

- a link redirecting to the questionnaire was published in a closed Facebook community group called "Tłumacze" (Translators);
- the contact with sworn translators of the Polish language was established through an e-mail invitation to the study (the e-mail contained a link to the questionnaire).

The first phase of the research was conducted using a two-way survey. Depending on the answer to the first question, respondents were taken to one of two separate questionnaires where they were to answer (anonymously) a series of questions regarding the ways in which they use CAT technology in their daily work. The questionnaires were prepared using Google Forms due to ease of access and data export (CSV). The responses were downloaded in CSV format and parsed using Microsoft Excel.

The resulting data was reviewed and analysed with SPSS statistics software. The analysis of the data was performed with the use of the following statistical tools, described here for both methodological and terminological purposes:

a) Bartlett's test – used to evaluate if the variances are equal across groups or samples (see Bartlett, 1937; Snedecor and Cochran, 1989);

b)   correlation coefficient – used to measure how strong a relationship is between two variables;

c)   correlation matrix – allows the researcher to visualise which pairs of data have the highest correlation. The correlation matrix computes the correlation coefficients of the columns of a matrix; it takes the form of a table showing correlation coefficients between sets of variables (NIST, 2013);

d)   Cronbach's (coefficient) alpha – a coefficient of reliability (or consistency) used to verify how closely related a set of items are as a group. It is considered to be a measure of scale reliability (UCLA: Statistical Consulting Group, 2020);

e)   diagonal matrix – used in process charting; a square matrix where off-diagonal entries are all equal to zero (Taboga, 2017);

f)   Kaiser criterion – the eigenvalue-greater-than-one rule; it involves dismissing all components with eigenvalues < 1.0 (Kaiser, 1960);

g)   Kaiser-Mayer-Olkin (KMO) test – used in research "to determine the sampling adequacy of data that are to be used for Factor Analysis" and to ensure that the variables used to measure a particular concept are measuring the concept intended (IBM, 2012);

h)   latent variable – any variable occurring in a statistical problem, which cannot be observed (Bartholomew, 2015);

i)   Mann-Whitney test – a nonparametric test "used to test whether two samples are likely to derive from the same population (i.e., that the two populations have the same shape)" (LaMorte, 2017);

j)   mean – the arithmetic mean, more commonly known as "the average," the sum of a list of numbers divided by the number of items on the list; useful in determining the overall trend of a data set or providing a rapid snapshot of the data;

k)   scree plot – used in "determining the number of factors to retain in factor analysis. With this procedure eigenvalues are plotted against their ordinal numbers, and one examines to find where a break or a levelling of the slope of the plotted line occurs" (Kanyongo, 2005: 122);

l)   skewness – a measure of the asymmetry of the probability distribution of a real-valued random variable about its mean, quantified to define the extent to which a distribution differs from a normal distribution;

m)   Spearman rank correlation coefficient – used to discover the strength, or the quality, of a link between two sets of data (see Spearman, 1904);

n)   standard deviation – a measure of a spread of data around the mean; a high standard deviation signifies that data is spread more widely from the mean, whereas a low standard deviation signals that more data align with the mean; useful for determining dispersion of data points;

o)   T-test – used to test hypotheses about the mean of a small sample; it is drawn from a normally distributed population when the population standard deviation remains unknown;

p)   Varimax rotation method – used "at one level of factor analysis as an attempt to clarify the relationship among factors" (Allen, 2017: 531).

5.1.3   Participants

The study takes into consideration such factors as age, language pairs, types of translated documents, attitude to machine translation, expectations regarding translator training, and more. The questionnaire was aimed primarily at full-time professional freelance translators. All of the participants have been in the translation business for at least ten years. Over 33% have been in the translation business for more than 20 years. Responses analysed in the study come from 141 professional translators working in the Polish language. There are 51 (36.5%) respondents who declare that they do not use CAT tools and 90 (63.5%) respondents who confirmed that they use CAT tools.

5.1.4   Limitations of the Study

Several limitations of the proposed study should be noted. The study was conducted using the CAWI (Computer-Assisted Web Interview) technique based on a questionnaire, which collected self-reported data. Collecting information through a self-report is subject to bias, so the data may be affected by data collection procedures. There is no guarantee that what the translators declared is actually true; nevertheless, the authors believe that there is no better means or methods of data collection for this particular kind of research. There was a strong sense of anonymity. The questions were very basic and job-specific, which served to fortify the dependability of the data. An important element of the study was to verify the experience of professional translators. This goal was achieved through validation of the survey. As a result, it was ensured that the interpretation of the findings was not impacted.

Another limitation that needs to be acknowledged is there is no guarantee that the same people were not present in both groups of respondents, but the authors see no reason why a translator would like to do the same questionnaire twice with no clear cause or purpose. Thus, the authors firmly believe that the aforementioned limitations do not affect the validity of the study, and the scope of the study is in no way limited. The findings show acceptable statistical reliability and validity (see chapter 6).

5.2   Attitudes Towards the Study

First, it seems fairly interesting to discuss feedback comments made on the survey and issues raised in the remarks of the respondents, mainly in relation to the interaction between the translation business and academia. A selection of comments reported in the study which reflect the attitude of some translators towards academia and fellow translators will be grouped and analysed later.

It needs to be noted that the majority of translators asked to participate in the study were enthusiastic about the idea of contributing to the research and thus were very helpful with providing the information that the authors requested. Nevertheless, a number of comments aired by some respondents are illustrative of peculiar issues worth investigating here.

All of those qualitative examples of comments were expressed incidentally by only a number of respondents as additional feedback. For discussion purposes, they have been tentatively grouped into three types, and it is suggested here that they represent different attitudes that respondents possess and display (i.e., hostile, dismissive, and humorous).

5.2.1   Hostile Tone: Generation Gap

The first group of comments that will be mentioned here is indicative of a rather hostile approach. It was a comment expressed by one of the freelance translators that sparked a discussion in which a number of other derogatory comments about the logical motivation behind helping in such research studies. As the respondents had been informed about the purpose of the study, they were aware of the authors' aim to use the findings so as to identify priorities and objectives for translator training.

The negative attitude that is sampled here involves an unwillingness to contribute to improving the state of translation education. Better educational solutions and opportunities for trainee translators would mean a potential increase in competitiveness within the already highly saturated translation market.

The discussion started with a very straightforward comment by one of the respondents [R1]; it was a remark made immediately after the survey was released and made available to the members of the closed group (see section 5.1). This rather uncompromisingly forthright observation reads as follows:

[R1]:   What's in it for us? Why should we care to help improve translator training programmes? It is much better for us when young translators are poorly educated.

Interestingly enough, although the comment was swiftly liked by one of the group members, another group member published a prompt replay which reads:

[R2]: Maybe just to have somebody to help us fight against the machines. . . . The young should be granted the same opportunities as we had when we were young.

Forceful and uplifting as this comment seemed, it was instantaneously returned with another remark:

[R3]: It's illogical. If the young are supposed to have the same opportunities, then why should we help them?

This short discussion continues for a while and ends with a confession by the author of the first comment and other similar comments which read:

[R1]: Maybe it is just my bitterness because I was never helped by anyone.
[R4]: And what chances did we have when we were young? There was no Google, no websites like proz.com, no other tools or opportunities which make the translator's work something completely different from what it was when we were young.

The whole conversation shows how much of a competitive rivalry is present in the translation business. The apparent outburst of resentment expressed in the first and the third comment implies that translators who are already established in the translation industry feel that they did not receive the proper translation training. As it is stated in the third comment, the respondent [R3] clearly means that if older translators were not granted the opportunity to use the knowledge of "fighting against the machines," then the young should not be helped and granted this opportunity either.

Moreover, the issue raised in the aforementioned short exchange of views also came up several times in the survey when respondents were asked to answer in their own words and thus did not have to limit themselves to pre-coded categories of answers. To exemplify, a selection of answers to an open question about the expectations of non-users towards translation programmes offered at universities follows:

- CAT tools should be introduced into translation programmes
- Such courses should give an introduction to CAT tools
- They such teach simple rules of using CAT tools in the Polish language
- a lot of practical classes on CAT tools
- showing why CAT tools are worth the investment
- I have no idea
- practice
- help in using CAT tools

- Hands-on experience
- Nothing because I don't want to use CAT tools
- an advanced IT course showing online access to various resources; a course in self-study
- practical learning to use CAT tools with particular attention to individual style which should be worked on by every translator. Because I don't use any tool, although I know the tools, it is hard to be more specific in answering this question. I believe they are helpful, but quite expensive. Still, as for me, working on the source text and then the target text in a traditional way brings much more satisfaction, and this means more than just "increasing your income"
- using the tools in the Polish language
- a decent training with a lot of practice and the access to one computer for every single student and not mainly the theory or short presentations. I took part in workshops by supposedly renowned companies, which were quite expensive, but their quality was disappointing and I got discouraged, maybe that is why I did not decide to buy and use the tools. It was almost 10 years ago so my age was not a problem and until now I am fairly computer literate so it is not the problem either. There are two factors that are crucial here: I work as a sworn translator of a rather rare language (Italian) and I work a full-time steady job so I can choose and freely decide about my payment, which is not a typical situation. In general, I think that CAT training should be an indispensable element of translation programmes at universities for students who are about to enter this more and more difficult translation market
- I expect universities to finally start teaching technical skills to translation students!
- Basic skills and maybe a comparison of different tools
- I would like the tools to be easy to use
- Hard to say
- Such translation programmes should be conducted by a software programmer or developer who would give young translators additional basic skills in programming CAT tools, which would allow them to develop their competences in other fields

The majority of respondents' comments listed here state that translation programmes should offer practical classes, so the prevailing assumption is that universities do not teach students any practical technological skills. The view expressed here touches upon a very important issue for translation teachers and curricula coordinators to reconsider. Many universities nowadays offer a lot of complex practical courses in CAT tool application, but still, it is a popular opinion that universities limit the programmes to theory only. It is clearly visible that translators have the impression of a gap between the translation industry and academia, which is a problem that needs addressing within translation education.

5.2.2 Humorous Tone: What About Bridging the Gap?

Some respondents made additional comments revealing a friendly and light attitude towards the study in which they were asked to participate and the "academic side" that its authors represent.

[R5]:   Please don't tell trainee translators about CAT tools, translation market is highly competitive :-)
[R6]:   I hope I will be invited to teach in those training programmes ;)

Despite the fact that both comments are meant to be funny, there is a hidden truth in these statements. What can be read from the remark made by one of the respondents [R5] is the anxiety of translators about their future career. The remark about "competitiveness" of the market is particularly interesting in the context of the CSA reports mentioned earlier in the course of the book, which clearly state that the demand for high-quality machine-assisted translation services is relatively high (see section 1.2). It shows that the local Polish market may seem oversaturated with translators or maybe some translators have difficulty taking full advantage of CAT tools (possibly because they were not taught how to use them in the first place).

5.2.3 Dismissive Tone: Market-Academia Gap

Another group of comments illustrates an attitude which seems slightly dismissive of the survey and the authors' overall attempt to conduct such a study as if the entire effort was doomed to failure. One of the respondents made a comment which read:

[R7]:   All right, I did this questionnaire for you, but please correct that typo
in the word "codzinnej" [everyday]

The spelling mistake was indeed present in one of the questions, but however embarrassed the authors are to admit their negligence and apologise for the mistake of a missing letter in the given word, it seems rather antagonistic on the part of the author of the comment to go to such an effort and publish a separate post about it. One more comment that can be classified as slightly dismissive is the one presented next:

[R8]:   First and foremost, there is no such thing as "TRADOS," it is called SDL Trados Studio

The comment refers to one of the questions meant to elicit information on what CAT tools the respondents use. One of the options on the list indeed read "Trados." The authors are aware of the fact that the full name of the current version of the software is called SDL Trados Studio (the name first appeared in the 2009 edition). However, the most common (and much shorter) name for this CAT tool is "Trados," and it can be used to refer to Trados 1–7, SDL Trados 2007, and SDL Trados Studio(s) 2009–2019. Therefore, the name "Trados" was meant to refer to the family of CAT tools developed by Trados GmbH and SDL plc company. This explanation was delivered via public channels to the person complaining about the issue. Since there were no further comments, the authors of the study assumed the explanation was satisfactory.

The comment was, however, followed by a short discussion in a similar tone, which ended with the following conclusion:

[R9]:   The questionnaire looks at our profession from behind the university teacher's desk

Although the observation is indeed very true, apparently it does not seem to be just a statement of fact. The remark appears to contain a hidden meaning and illustrates a broader and quite pressing issue of the apparent gap between the translation market and academia. Universities continue to be perceived as lagging behind the translation market with its technological developments and innovations. Regrettably, the stereotypical generalisation that universities fail to prepare translators to enter the market prevails.

While it may still be true in the case of a number of educational programmes, the vast majority of translation curricula are becoming increasingly in line with the recent trends and the skill set required to work as a professional translation service provider. CAT technology has found its way into universities, and it is no longer taught only in a theoretical manner but oftentimes – as it is the case of the University of Łódź, Poland – courses in translation technology are offered within translation programmes and conducted by certified CAT tool trainers. There is an international trend to invest in technology-based translator training in order to meet the market needs (Doherty, 2016).

On the other hand, the question arises, when it comes to the problem of bridging the gap between the market and academia, whether this technological component is not overvalued nowadays. Intensive technological training may really not be that necessary, especially if it was supposed to be offered at the expense of other crucial components. As stated by Rodríguez de Céspedes (2017: 1), "efforts have been made to bridge the gap, but, according to recent studies, graduates still seem to be lacking certain professional service provision skills that are needed in industry." According to Pym (2003: 481), discussing the competences that translation trainees need, we will always be "one or two steps behind market demands." Although the authors of the present book are staunch supporters of providing students with the technological toolkit (see section 3.3), it needs to be emphasised that too much focus on technical skills could be wrong, given that CAT tools evolve and one tool is quickly replaced with a better solution. When it comes to translator training, it needs to be well-balanced so as not to deprive translation trainees of training in other vital skills that translation trainees need to acquire and that are much harder for them to learn on their own.

Furthermore, far beyond the problem with the scope of translation curriculum, it is worth considering here – in relation to the comment quoted earlier [R9] – what exactly is wrong in "looking at the profession from behind the university teacher's desk"? The relationship between industry and academia is fairly peculiar; although it is largely symbiotic, the cooperation between them appears to have been experiencing many limitations. The industry expects academia to identify the needs of the market and immediately implement necessary measures into translation programmes. Nevertheless, the university needs to maintain its research capacity, so it must stay dedicated to developing research and not compromise its values and priorities. Although both university and industry have similar aims in the case of translation studies, the full potential of their collaboration is far from being utilised.

As much as the university wants to help the industry develop better translation programmes, it is also dependent on numerous external factors, such as restrictive internal policies or the relationship between higher education and government. The inability of marking its strengths in the translation industry is very often caused by certain procedures which regrettably hinder successful innovation. Nevertheless, studies such as the one presented here intend to strengthen the ties between the university and industry. Therefore, since better university-industry collaboration would surely have a beneficial impact on the translation market, any attempt at researching the market should at least be recognised. Mutual respect would definitely help to build a fruitful relationship between the two as well as to identify and implement further scopes of improvements in the field of translation.

References

Allen, Mike. (2017). *The Sage Encyclopedia of Communication Research Methods*. Vols. 1–4. Thousand Oaks, CA: SAGE Publications, Inc. https://doi.org/10.4135/9781483381411

Bartholomew, David J. (2015). Factor Analysis and Latent Structure Analysis: Overview. In Wright, James D. (ed.), *International Encyclopedia of the Social & Behavioral Sciences*. 2nd ed. Amsterdam: Elsevier, pp. 691–697.

Bartlett, Maurice S. (1937). Properties of Sufficiency and Statistical Tests. Proceedings of the Royal Statistical Society, Series A (160). *Mathematical and Physical Sciences*. Vol. 160, No. 901, May 18, 1937, pp. 268–282. JSTOR 96803 (https://jstor.org/stable/96803)

Chan, Sin-Wei. (2004). *A Dictionary of Translation Technology*. Hong Kong: The Chinese University Press.

Doherty, Stephen. (2016). The Impact of Translation Technologies on the Process and Product of Translation. *International Journal of Communication*, vol. 10, pp. 947–969.

IBM. (2012). *How-to Guide for IBM® SPSS® Statistics Software* [Online]. Available at: https://methods.sagepub.com/dataset/howtoguide/kmo-nilt-2012 (Accessed: 16 February 2020).

Kaiser, Henry F. (1960). The Application of Electronic Computers to Factor Analysis. *Educational and Psychological Measurement*, vol. 20, pp. 141–151. http://doi.org/10.1177/001316446002000116

Kanyongo, Gibbs Y. (2005). Determining the Correct Number of Components to Extract From a Principal Components Analysis: A Monte Carlo Study of the Accuracy of the Scree Plot. *Journal of Modern Applied Statistical Methods*, vol. 4(1), pp. 120–133.

LaMorte, Wayne W. (2017). *Mann Whitney U Test (Wilcoxon Rank Sum Test)*. Boston: University School of Public Health [Online]. Available at: http://sphweb.bumc.bu.edu/otlt/mph-modules/bs/bs704_nonparametric/BS704_Nonparametric4.html (Accessed: 16 February 2020).

National Institute of Standards and Technology (NIST). (2013). *Correlation Matrix* [Online]. Available at: www.itl.nist.gov/div898/software/dataplot/refman2/auxillar/corrmatr.htm (Accessed: 16 February 2020).

Pym, Anthony. (2003). Redefining Translation Competence in an Electronic Age. In Defence of a Minimalist Approach. *META*, vol. XLVIII(4), pp. 481–497.

Rodríguez de Céspedes, Begoña. (2017). Addressing Employability and Enterprise Responsibilities in the Translation Curriculum. *The Interpreter and Translator Trainer*, vol. 11(2–3), pp. 107–122. https://doi.org/10.1080/1750399X.2017.1344816

Snedecor, George W. and Cochran, William G. (1989). *Statistical Methods*. 8th ed. Ames: Iowa State University Press.

Spearman, Charles. (1904). The Proof and Measurement of Association Between Two Things. *American Journal of Psychology*, vol. 15(1), pp. 72–101. https://doi.org/10.2307/1412159

Taboga, Marco. (2017). *Lectures on Probability Theory and Mathematical Statistics.* 3rd ed. Scotts Valley, CA: CreateSpace Independent Publishing Platform.

UCLA: Statistical Consulting Group. (2020). *What Does Cronbach's Alpha Mean? UCLA: Statistical Consulting Group* [Online]. Available at: https://stats.idre.ucla. edu/other/mult-pkg/faq/general/faq-how-do-i-cite-web-pages-and-programs-from-the-ucla-statistical-consulting-group/ (Accessed: 16 February 2020).

6   Analysis of the Findings

Overview of the Chapter

This chapter discusses the results of the study conducted on both users and non-users of CAT software in Poland. Although the scope of the study is limited to the Polish context, it is to a large extent universal since the example of the Polish translation market can illustrate the reasons behind the reluctance of some professional translators to use CAT tools, their failure to use them efficiently or to make use of all the features available to address their clients' expectations better. The findings of the study help to identify the needs of the translation market and improve strategies used in translator training. This chapter presents the results, reviewed and analysed with SPSS statistics software. The statistical analysis of the data is supported with graphical representation of the findings. The chapter covers such aspects of the study as sample characteristics of the test subjects (section 6.1), usage of CAT tools (section 6.2) and machine translation (section 6.3), influence of CAT technology on income (section 6.4), individual evaluation of CAT tools by both CAT users and non-users (section 6.5), as well as reasons for using or not using CAT tools (section 6.6).

6.1   Sample Characteristics

As regards sample characteristics, 55 people (39.0%) belong to age groups 30–40 and 40–50 years. A total of 31 respondents fall into the 50+ age group. In terms of work experience, the majority of respondents reported between 20 and 30 years of experience. However, every third person in the study reported over 20 years of experience, while every fifth person reported less than ten years.

Due to its objectives, the study was conducted on two groups: CAT (computer-assisted translation) tools' users and people who previously did not use the software in their work (CAT non-users). The study involved 90 people from the first group (using CAT) and 51 from the other.

Table 6.1 The use of CAT tools and work experience

CAT tools		Work experience			Total
		Under 10 years	10–20 years	Over 20 years	
Are not used	n	4	25	22	51
	%	7.8%	49.0%	43.1%	100.0%
Are used	n	24	41	25	90
	%	26.7%	45.6%	27.8%	100.0%
Total	n	28	66	47	141
	%	19.9%	46.8%	33.3%	100.0%

Over 80% of CAT users are less than 50 years old, half of which are people between 30 and 40 years of age. In the case of people who do not use CAT tools, approximately two-thirds are aged 50 years or less. About half of those are between 40 and 50 years old.

Similar conclusions can be drawn in terms of work experience. Nearly half of CAT non-users have been working in the profession for over 20 years, and only 8% less than ten years. When it comes to people with work experience of ten years, the proportion of CAT users and non-users is similar (Table 6.1).

Based on the outlined data, it is possible to propose a relation between age, or work experience, and interest in the software. Younger people, with less work experience, were more drawn to it. On the other hand, people aged 60+ were least inclined to use it.

The majority of the respondents (84 subjects, 60%) use only one foreign language in their work (Table 6.4). Usually, it is English (68%) or – more rarely – German (21%) and French.

Thirty-two people (23%) use two languages at work; 16 people (11%) use three. Six people reported more than three languages. CAT users do not differ significantly at the same time (p = 0.729) from CAT non-users. The median value for both groups is 1, and the mean is 1.71 for CAT users and 1.65 for CAT non-users, respectively.

The two groups do not differ significantly in terms of the languages they use at work. However, it is worth noting that the CAT non-users less frequently use English (49% vs 79%) and more frequently use Russian (17.6%), French (15.7%), and Italian (9.8%). Only CAT users reported using such languages as Czech and Slovak (five persons); Croatian and Swedish (two persons); Finnish, Bulgarian, and Serbian (one person). In contrast, the CAT non-users reported using Greek, Portuguese, and Danish (one person) – not used by the CAT users (for a discussion of the results see chapter 7).

In both groups (p = 0.759) translations are conducted from Polish and into Polish, with a slight predominance of translations into Polish. The data indicate the usefulness of CAT tools in a situation where translation is the main source of income. Seventy-five per cent of CAT users live off translation, whereas in the case of CAT non-users, the number is 41%. In this regard, the differences are statistically significant (p < 0.001*). This tendency suggests that CAT tools enable translators to translate more and, therefore, support themselves financially based only on translation services.

In the case of orders carried out by CAT users, nearly half of the documents to be translated are editable. In the case of CAT non-users, only 25% of the content is editable. They mostly work on non-editable documents (49%) and do not receive translation packages. In this regard, the differences are statistically significant (p < 0.001*). The authors assumed that the choice to use CAT tools would be easier for those translators whose jobs involve editable documents as opposed to those translators who deal predominantly with non-editable ones, which would require time and effort to prepare them for CAT tools. The data confirm this assumption.

When it comes to the use of CAT tools in the past or the planned future, it is worth noting that 29% of non-users have tried using the tools before. In contrast, when asked if they want to use CAT tools in the future, only one-fourth of the respondents were positive. One-third have no plans to use them, and the majority (43%, 22 respondents) have no definite opinion on the issue.

6.2   Usage

CAT users (n = 90) were asked for additional information about the ways in which they use the CAT software. Thirty per cent of CAT users feel the need to use several tools in their work. However, almost half of the respondents reported using more than one tool (44 people, 49.8% of the CAT users; see Table 6.2). Primarily, they indicate SDL Trados Studio (20 in 44 respondents) or memoQ (15 in 44 respondents). Other tools mentioned included Wordfast (four people), MateCat or Open Language Tools (one person each), or other tools (two persons). Twenty-six people (28.9%) reported using two CAT tools; ten people (11.1%) use three, although there were also people (three in total) who use at least five CAT tools.

SDL Trados Studio is by far the most popular CAT tool – it is used by nearly half of the respondents (Table 6.7). The second and third places were taken by memoQ (29.1%) and Wordfast (10.6%). Other choices included Memsource, Across, and XTM (5–6% of respondents). Individual respondents mentioned such tools as MateCat, Open Language Tools, Star Transit, Wordbee, DejaVu, SmartCat, and OmegaT as well. What is more, nearly one in ten people still use other tools (Table 6.2). It should be noted that

Table 6.2 The use of specific CAT tools

CAT tools	Number of people	%
SDL Trados Studio	61	43.3
memoQ	41	29.1
Wordfast	15	10.6
Memsource	9	6.4
Across	8	5.7
XTM	8	5.7
MateCat	5	3.5
Open Language Tools	4	2.8
Star Transit	2	1.4
Wordbee	2	1.4
DejaVu	1	0.7
SmartCat	1	0.7
OmegaT	1	0.7
Other	13	9.2

such tools as Wordbee, Star Transit, SmartCat, and OmegaT are used only alongside other CAT tools (by users who use at least three different tools).

In the case of the majority of CAT users (91.1%), the CAT tools in use are their property. Every fourth person is granted access to the tool for the duration of the project. Rarely, access is granted for an indefinite period.

It has to be noted that only two respondents have been granted a licence to a client's CAT tool for an indefinite period, and only five for the duration of the project. Two respondents use both forms of licencing, while another three own their own licence as well. Of all the CAT tools used in work, two-thirds are owned by their users. The data are consistent with the idea that the CAT-based translation industry in Poland is decentralised (i.e., most free-lancers carry out individual CAT-based projects instead of receiving them from large LSPs) (see the following).

The majority of respondents (43%) receive orders from their clients in the form of editable files. One-fourth of CAT users receive translation packages. Less common are editable documents which require editing of the layout in order to prepare it for translation, or non-editable documents which need to be prepared completely for translation in CAT tools. Those figures show that CAT-based translation is not that mature in Poland, yet 25% of trans-lators working with translation packages means that LSPs do not require CAT tools to such an extent[1] as the popularity of CAT tools might suggest. Therefore, it can be concluded that CAT tools are the conscious choice of their users, who see financial benefits in using them.

Every third CAT user (34.4%) confirmed using machine translation (e.g., Microsoft Translator in Memsource) results while working in the CAT environment. Every third CAT user frequently or very frequently uses translation memories provided by the client. Half of the respondents do so rarely or very rarely. Given the number of responses collected, the data support the idea that around a third of CAT users carry out package-based projects for LSPs, while the rest does so infrequently if at all.

CAT users are rather satisfied with the quality of resources provided by the customer (40% vs 27% who find them problematic). However, if we consider that 33% of respondents have no opinion on the issue, the overall picture is one of "mixed feelings" about the issue. Such distribution of results suggests that the quality of resources is indeed a problem, especially when we consider that almost a third of the entire group reports them to be unsatisfactory. This may support the claim that CAT tools are not yet that widespread among LSPs in Poland and, as a result, LSP side handling of resources leaves much room for improvement.

The data collected through the survey suggest that almost 90% of users experienced issues with CAT compatibility in the past (almost 70% of them frequently). The issues may relate to a translation package, translation memory, or termbase incompatibility. As a result, translators have to work on the same (or most compatible) CAT tools, which discourages competition on the market and favours SDL Trados Studio, the CAT tools with the greatest chunk of the market. It is clearly an area for improvement for software developers.

Despite these problems, the vast majority of CAT users confirm the usefulness of these tools. Ninety per cent of them agree that CAT tools have influenced their translation efficiency in a positive way. The positive influence was strongly confirmed by more than half of the respondents. Most of the respondents (90%) believe that the increase in the efficiency of translation when using CAT tools was worth the time and money spent to buy the software and learn how to use it. Only 4% of respondents are of a different opinion. It proves that CAT tools fulfil their designed role.

Most CAT users (93%) plan to purchase CAT software again in the future (5% of those are going to change the CAT tool). Some users plan to abandon them and return to traditional translation (7%). The data reinforce previous findings regarding satisfaction with CAT software. Few translators see the need to change the tool they use.

6.3   Machine Translation

CAT users have very polarised opinions on machine translation. Nearly half of them believe that machine translation is a competition for all translators. On the other hand, 41% of respondents believe that they are of no consequence from the point of view of a professional translator since a human will always translate better than a machine. Those who perceive machine translation as a threat only to CAT non-users, or only to those who do use MT, are much fewer. It cannot be determined what lies behind both views. One can assume that it is closely related to the degree of exposure to MT-based translation (as post-editors, for example) and the awareness of its current quality. Definitely, this is an area to be further explored in the future.

6.4 Income

Since rates provided by translators differ considerably in many respects (price, unit, currency, range, language), the analysis of the actual income of the respondents required establishing a unification system. A "word" has been selected as the basic price unit in the case of CAT users (since CAT systems use words for analysis and quote purposes) and characters with spaces in the case of non-CAT users (most common price unit for non-CAT translations).

Considering all of the differences, it was assumed that an approach focused on the average rate/price would be the most valid. Therefore, if a translator provided rates from the foreign language into Polish and from Polish into the foreign language, an average was calculated. If only one translation direction was mentioned, it was used in the study (under the assumption that this translator does not translate in the opposite direction). Similarly, if a price range was given, the median was used. If prices were provided in foreign currencies, they were converted to PLN based on the average exchange rate published by the National Bank of Poland (as of 12 May 2019).

In the case of CAT users who provided their prices per number of characters with spaces, values have been converted to a price per word using the following values: 240 words per 1,800 characters with spaces in a random, continuous legal text in Polish. It can be argued that the same number of characters with spaces will result in a bit different number of words depending on a language, but the anonymity of responses to the study results in the inability to align the price and the given language, especially considering the fact that some translators work in more than two languages. Therefore, the number of words in the Polish text has been used with regard to the fact that it was the language common to all respondents.

In the case of non-CAT users who provided their rates based on words, rather than characters with spaces, the price was converted to characters with spaces following the same (albeit reversed) principle.

When the price was given per 1,125 or 1,600 characters with spaces, it was first recalculated as per 1,800 characters with spaces and then converted to the word-based rate. At the same time, if no page size/volume was given, it was assumed that the page measures 1,800 characters with spaces.

CAT users, as opposed to CAT non-users, rarely differentiate among rates depending on the direction of translation. Such a procedure is customary to two-thirds of CAT users and only to one-fifth of CAT non-users. CAT non-users are more likely (80%) to charge more for translation jobs into a foreign language. Higher rates when translating into their native language are rarely used (as indicated by only 2% of CAT users).

Participants of the study were asked to provide information regarding their remuneration. It was an optional question answered by 41 CAT users and 24 CAT non-users (interestingly, that amounts to about 50% of respondents in both groups).

The data show that the current remuneration of translators in both groups is mostly the same (Figure 6.1; the Mann-Whitney test score is $p = 0.946$). It can be seen, however, that the remuneration gap is slightly higher in the case of CAT non-users (whiskers are slightly longer), especially at the upper levels of rates. The analysis of statistics (Table 6.3) allows us to conclude that the average rate in the two groups reaches approximately 0.21 PLN per word, and half of the respondents translate for a rate not lower than 0.19 PLN (0.185 in the case of CAT users). The rates of individual translators vary from the average by an average of approximately 0.08 PLN (0.0794 for CAT users and 0.0849 for CAT non-users). In both groups, the rates are

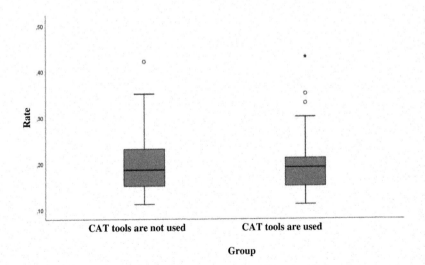

Figure 6.1 Comparison of rates for the translation (in PLN per word)

Table 6.3 The level of remuneration of CAT and non-CAT translators

CAT tools	Are used	Are not used
Number of replies	24	41
Minimum	0.11	0.11
Maximum	0.42	0.43
Average	**0.2075**	**0.2090**
5% trimmed mean	0.2017	0.2022
Median	0.1850	0.1900
Standard deviation	0.0794	0.0849
Range	0.31	0.32
Interquartile range	0.08	0.08
Skewness	1.235	1.425
Kurtosis	0.977	1.456

Table 6.4 Evaluation of CAT tools and the number of languages used by translators in their work vs the rate

CAT tools			CAT	CAT1	CAT2	Number of languages
Are not used	Rate	rho	0.218	0.061	0.212	0.810
		p	0.305	0.778	0.319	<0,001
Are used	Rate	rho	0.097	0.098	0.141	0.120
		p	0.545	0.543	0.378	0.455

Note: rho – Spearman rank correlation coefficient; p – dependency statistically significant ($\alpha = 0.05$).

characterised by a strong positive skew (i.e., rates not in excess of the average are more common).

The value of the rate is not related to the evaluation of CAT tools (for both analysed groups). However, it is closely related to the number of languages that the translators use. The relationship is strongly positive (i.e., translators who utilise more languages get significantly higher rates) (Table 6.4). However, this applies only to CAT non-users. In the case of CAT users, this tendency is not statistically significant (p = 0.455). Interestingly, it has a negative direction (knowledge of more languages does not support higher rates and vice versa; however, the tendency is not too clear, and it is difficult to generalise regarding the entire population in this respect).

Respondents also gave their thoughts on the relationship between the use of CAT tools and remuneration levels. More than two-thirds of CAT users confirmed that the use of CAT tools affected their income (according to 40% in a definitive way). Meanwhile, CAT non-users see little opportunity for increased financial benefits due to the use of CAT tools. Such an opinion is shared by nearly 25% of the CAT non-users (the percentage is similar to the group who does not believe in positive effects of CAT tools), while nearly half of the respondents do not have a clear opinion in this regard. On the other hand, over half of CAT non-users are pleased with the level of their wages. However, almost the same number again is of the opposite opinion (Table 6.5). Those satisfied with their income are a little less optimistic in terms of raising their remuneration through the use of CAT tools (the correlation is negative, although statistically not significant: rho = –0.121, p = 0.398).

6.5   CAT Tools Evaluation

In general, the opinion regarding CAT tools is definitely better amongst those who use them (in contrast to non-users). The same applies to the majority of areas (Table 6.5). Only the risk of duplication of erroneous TM suggestions is similarly evaluated by both groups. Large similarity is also observed in the case of the assessment of how income is limited due to the fact that only the part of the document that was actually translated is taken into account. The similarity also lies in the perception of how the software helps to manage projects. However (as is suggested by p being only slightly greater than the level of significance), the differences here are greater.

The analysis of both the value of arithmetic means and median shows that CAT users appreciate the software because it helps to assure consistency of the translation, speeds up the translation process, and allows the user to effectively manage terminology (median at level 5; average approximately 4.4). Both price and the fact that they carry a risk of duplication of erroneous suggestions (e.g., from external translation memories and terminology databases) were considered the biggest negative of CAT tools. CAT non-users are also anxious about the fact that CAT tools reduce remuneration due to the fact that only the portion of the document that was actually translated is actually paid for.

It should also be emphasised that a considerable part of CAT non-users has no definite opinion in this regard. More than half of CAT users see no problem in the fact that these solutions necessitate text segmentation, which may have a negative effect on the style of translation. However, more than a third of the group (as opposed to 25% of the CAT non-users) noticed the problem. Seventy-five per cent of CAT users (as compared to 20% of CAT non-users) deny that the software results in repeatability of translations and negatively affects the development of translator skills. On the other hand,

Table 6.5 CAT tools evaluation

CAT tools		Average		Median		p
		Are not used	Are used	Are not used	Are used	
C1	Force text segmentation, which may have a negative effect on the style of translation	2.78	3.32	3.00	4.00	0.007
C2	Carry the risk of reusing incorrect matches (e.g., from external translation memories and termbases)	2.55	2.89	3.00	2.00	0.341
C3	Force repeatability of translation, while limiting the development of translator	2.86	3.81	3.00	4.00	<0,001*
C4	Are expensive	2.37	2.88	3.00	3.00	0.045
C5	Are complicated to use	2.76	3.71	3.00	4.00	<0,001*
C6	Limit salary due to the fact that only the part of the document subject to translation is paid for	2.55	3.06	3.00	3.00	0.054
C7	Allow users to speed up the translation process	3.71	4.43	4.00	5.00	<0,001*
C8	Increase the number of orders	3.22	3.66	3.00	4.00	0.015
C9	Facilitate retaining consistency of translations	3.71	4.44	4.00	5.00	<0,001*
C10	Allow users to effectively manage terminology	3.55	4.32	4.00	5.00	<0,001*
C11	Give instant access to machine translation (through plugins)	3.16	3.66	3.00	4.00	0.001*
C12	Facilitate order management	3.12	3.40	3.00	3.00	0.056
C13	Increase salary as a result of increasing the volume of translated text	3.04	3.61	3.00	4.00	<0,001*

Note: Questions C1–C6 were reverse-coded for the purposes of determining the statistics.

p – probability in Mann-Whitney test, *statistically significant differences ($\alpha = 0.05$).

40% of CAT non-users claim otherwise.[2] The majority of CAT users do not confirm the handling difficulty of the software. Twenty-five per cent of CAT users and 40% of CAT non-users claim otherwise. In terms of wage reduction, two-thirds of CAT non-users had no definite opinion on the issue. An equal number of CAT users confirms and denies the issue.

Seventy per cent of CAT users confirm the speed boost to the translation process and an increase in the coherence of translations. About 10% of CAT users do not acknowledge such advantages – significantly more than in the case of CAT non-users. Every fourth user sees no impact on the number of orders, while 60% confirm this advantage of CAT tools.

Almost all CAT users (and half of CAT non-users) recognise the strengths of effective terminology management; half of those strongly support this claim. Almost 75% of CAT non-users (and 20–37% of CAT users) had no definite opinion regarding immediate access to machine translation, order management, and salary increase due to increased work effectiveness. In contrast, about 50% of CAT users are positive about those aspects.

When making a synthetic evaluation of CAT tools, a CAT Indicator (CATI) was built. It was determined as the total of the points obtained for 13 questions on the scale (questions C1–C6 have been previously transcoded vice versa). This indicator has high reliability – Cronbach's coefficient alpha is at 0.813. The results of the exploratory factor analysis indicated that the scale is not uniform. Two subscales can be indicated, as is suggested by the scree chart (Figure 6.2) and the results obtained using the Kaiser method (eigenvalue greater than one refers to two factors). Both the Kaiser-Mayer-Olkin

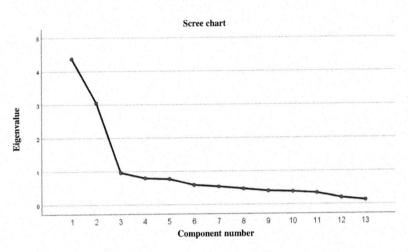

Scree chart

Figure 6.2 Scree chart for the CAT tools evaluation scale

(KMO) (0.848) and Bartlett's test for sphericity results ($\chi^2(78) = 877,450$; $p < 0,001*$) confirm that the set of variables has been selected properly.

What is more, the values of the coefficients on the diagonal matrix, inverse to the correlation matrix (smaller than ten), confirm the proper relationship between the partial variables (scale items). The first factor explains approximately 34% of the variation in the latent variable, and the second 23% (both jointly explain 57% of the variation, which is a satisfactory result).

In the case of all variables, factor loadings are greater than 0.5 (and even 0.6), which confirms the high significance of each of the elements in the CAT evaluation. The first of the extracted factors plays a greater role from the point of view of measuring the CAT tool evaluation. It can be described as "CAT strengths." From the point of view of measuring the CAT evaluation, the most important aspects in this group are: "they enable effective terminology management," "they facilitate retaining consistency of translations," and "they allow to speed up the translation process" (Table 6.6). The

Table 6.6 Results of exploratory factor analysis

CAT tools	Component	
	1	*2*
Allow users to manage terminology effectively	**0.894**	0.020
Facilitate retaining consistency of translations	**0.867**	−0.059
Allow users to speed up the translation process	**0.844**	−0.070
Give instant access to machine translation (through plugins)	**0.705**	0.037
Increase the number of orders	**0.684**	0.106
Increase salary as a result of increasing the volume of the translated text	**0.677**	0.129
Facilitate order management	**0.652**	0.115
Carry the risk of reusing incorrect matches (e.g., from external translation memories and termbases)	−0.070	**0.799**
Force text segmentation, which may have a negative effect on the style of the translation	0.102	**0.738**
Are complicated to use	0.259	**0.715**
Limit salary due to the fact that only the part of the document subject to translation is paid for	−0.086	**0.709**
Force repeatability of translation while limiting the development of the translator	0.173	**0.706**
Are expensive	−0.039	**0.669**
Percentage of explained variance	33.66	57.13
Cronbach's coefficient alpha for subscale	0.877	0.820

group also includes questions that allow us to evaluate them in terms of giving access to machine translation, increasing the number of orders and remuneration, as well as a project management feature. In turn, the second subscale consists of elements that can be described as "CAT weaknesses." Their connection with the factor, while weaker than for the strengths, is still high – the highest for the risk of reusing incorrect matches (e.g., from external translation memories and termbases) and, subsequently, forcing text segmentation, which can negatively affect the style of the translation.

Synthetic sub-indicators CAT1 ("CAT strengths") and CAT2 ("CAT weaknesses") are also characterised by high reliability – Cronbach's alpha coefficient reaches 0.877 and 0.820, respectively. The factors have been isolated using the principal components method. The Varimax rotation method was used.

When comparing a synthetic evaluation of CAT – in total and within the boundaries of subscales (Figure 6.3) – it can be seen that CAT users achieve significantly higher scores than non-users. At the same time, there

CAT tools:	Are used	Are not used
Number of replies	24	41
Minimum	0.11	0.11
Maximum	0.42	0.43
Average	**0.2075**	**0.2090**
5% trimmed mean	0.2017	0.2022
Median	0.1850	0.1900
Standard deviation	0.0794	0.0849
Range	0.31	0.32
Interquartile range	0.08	0.08
Skewness	1.235	1.425
Kurtosis	0.977	1.456

Figure 6.3 Comparison of CAT tools evaluation indicators

are people among CAT users who are less positive about the strengths of CAT tools. In the case of CAT non-users, the evaluation is both positive and negative.

Average evaluation of CAT tools is approximately eight points higher in CAT users vs non-users. This rating is generally high for CAT users, with a low degree of asymmetry (results above average are slightly more frequent) and a relatively low standard deviation (SD = 8.67). Results of half of the most typical respondents in this group differ by a maximum of ten points. The results are even more homogeneous (with low skewness and concentration of distribution) in the case of CAT non-users (lower evaluation). The evaluation of strengths and weaknesses is higher in the case of CAT users, also with a stronger diversity of this group (Table 6.7).

If we take age into account while conducting a general CAT assessment, the main effect of the "group" factor remains statistically significant (assuming a fixed age by convention, group membership significantly differentiates the CAT rating ($p < 0.001*$, $\eta^2 = 0.107$)). In turn, the significance of age ($p = 0.694$, $\eta^2 = 0.011$) as well as its interaction ($p = 0.542$, $\eta^2 = 0.016$) is not statistically significant. Similar conclusions apply to the discussed relations, including seniority – for the main effect of the group ($p < 0.001*$, $\eta^2 = 0.147$), for age ($p = 0.949$, $\eta^2 = 0.001$), for interaction ($p = 0.538$, $\eta^2 = 0.009$). As can be seen, the strength of the effect is higher if we conventionally assume constant seniority (rather than age).

Table 6.7 Descriptive statistics for CAT tools evaluation indicators in CAT users and non-users

CAT tools	CAT		CAT1		CAT2	
	Are not used	*Are used*	*Are not used*	*Are used*	*Are not used*	*Are used*
Range of variation	13 ÷ 65		7 ÷ 35		6 ÷ 30	
Minimum	30.00	13.00	13.00	7.00	6.00	6.00
Maximum	50.00	65.00	33.00	35.00	28.00	30.00
Average	39.37	47.19	23.49	27.52	15.88	19.67
5% trimmed mean	39.30	47.55	23.38	28.10	15.79	19.77
Median	39.00	47.00	23.00	29.00	16.00	20.00
Standard deviation	4.59	8.67	3.44	6.16	4.01	5.67
Range	20.00	52.00	20.00	28.00	22.00	24.00
Interquartile range	6.00	10.00	4.00	7.00	4.00	7.00
Skewness	0.288	−0.854	0.419	−1.431	0.333	−0.105
Kurtosis	−0.039	2.586	1.905	2.235	2.109	−0.339

The average CAT rating differs the most for translators with the lowest seniority (up to ten years) and the youngest (between 30 and 50 years of age) – here the difference between CAT users and non-users (in favour of the former) is the most significant. In turn, people over 60 years of age are very similar (Figures 6.4–6.5).

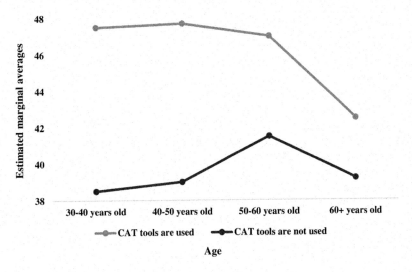

Figure 6.4 Overall CAT evaluation by CAT usage and age

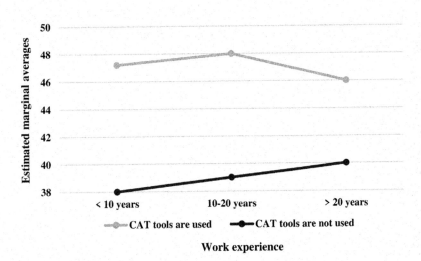

Figure 6.5 Overall CAT evaluation by CAT usage and work experience

The assessment of CAT tools in both groups is not significantly related to the number of languages used (Table 6.8). It can be noticed that, within the sample, CAT weaknesses are more noticed by translators who use more languages (the correlation coefficient is positive but not statistically significant, and this relation is more pronounced for CAT users). On the other hand, CAT strengths are more clearly perceived by translators focusing on a smaller number of languages (here the correlation coefficient is negative but still statistically insignificant, and the relation is slightly more pronounced for CAT non-users). The overall rating is positively correlated with the number of languages in the case of CAT users and negatively correlated for the other group.

The results presented in Table 6.9 also testify to the different perception of CAT tools by their users and non-users. Slightly more than

Table 6.8 The number of languages used by translators vs CAT evaluation

CAT tools			*CAT*	*CAT1*	*CAT2*
Are not used	The number of languages	rho	−0.166	−0.133	0.036
		p	0.244	0.352	0.800
Are used	The number of languages	rho	0.094	−0.037	0.149
		p	0.377	0.732	0.161

Note: rho – Spearman rank correlation coefficient; p – dependency statistically significant ($\alpha = 0.05$).

Table 6.9 Answers to the question: "Which phrase best reflects your opinion on CAT tools?"

CAT tools		*Are used*	*Are not used*
Additional difficulty	Number	1	2
	%	1.1%	3.9%
A necessity, when we think about the future	Number	26	6
	%	28.9%	11.8%
Powerful, albeit expensive tool	Number	10	11
	%	11.1%	21.6%
Waste of time and money	Number	2	4
	%	2.2%	7.8%
Bullseye from the perspective of a professional translator	Number	50	0
	%	55.6%	0.0%
I have no opinion	Number	1	28
	%	1.1%	54.9%
Total	Number	90	51
	%	100.0%	100.0%

half of CAT users consider them a top choice (a sentiment shared by none of the respondents from the other group). In turn, slightly more than half of those CAT non-users have no opinion on the topic. Looking from a perspective, 25% of CAT users and 12% of CAT non-users consider the software a necessity. In the case of CAT non-users, the most frequently mentioned term was "powerful, albeit expensive tool" (approximately 22% of CAT users against approximately 11% of CAT non-users).

6.6 Reasons for Using or Not Using CAT Tools

The respondents have chosen CAT tools based primarily on their own decision supported by market research and/or customer requirements. Opinions of other translators and/or educational experiences were also important (as suggested by about 30% of the respondents).

Frequently, the choice of CAT tools is conditioned by several factors (however, about half of the respondents indicated only one reason). Most often, their own decision is supported by market research followed by customer requirements, education, or the opinions of other translators. Translators who have chosen CAT tools due to the client's requirements simultaneously followed the opinions of other translators and took price into consideration. Free access to the software (as part of the project) or purchase price (e.g., discount) were not the only criteria for selection. Those who indicated free access, most often associated it with education or customer requirement. On the other hand, those who indicated price associated it with their own decision supported by market research (Table 6.10).

The reasons for not using CAT tools are also diverse. Half of the respondents who do not use CAT software do not feel such a need. What is more, the share of people for whom the price of these tools is too high, as well as those who do not have clients who require the use of CAT tools, is similar (~40%). Twenty-five per cent of respondents reported the fact that the tools are too complicated to use. Other reasons were less frequently mentioned. Table 6.11 presents that the use of CAT was most often prevented by the coexistence of several factors, including the high price with no customer demand, in particular. People anxious about the limitations of the language creativity of the translator, as well as the protection of confidential data, most often pointed to the lack of need to use the tools.

Table 6.10 Combination of CAT selection criteria

CAT tools	Education	Client's requirement	Opinions of other translators	Purchase price	Own decision, based on market research	Free access as part of a project
Client's requirement	7					
Opinions of other translators	4	10				
Purchase price	6	9	5			
Own decision, based on market research	12	14	10	8		
Free access as part of a project	4	3	2	1	2	
Other	2	2	0	0	1	1

Table 6.11 Combination of criteria for not using CAT tools

CAT tools	I have no such need	The price of CAT tools is too high	CAT tools are too complicated to use	I don't have clients who require the use of CAT tools	CAT tools limit the translator's language creativity	I have concerns about the protection of confidential data
The price of CAT tools is too high	8					
CAT tools are too complicated to use	5	8				
I don't have clients who require the use of CAT tools	8	10	4			

(*Continued*)

Table 6.11 (Continued)

CAT tools	I have no such need	The price of CAT tools is too high	CAT tools are too complicated to use	I don't have clients who require the use of CAT tools	CAT tools limit the translator's language creativity	I have concerns about the protection of confidential data
CAT tools limit the translator's language creativity	5	4	2	2		
I have concerns about the protection of confidential data	4	1	2	3	1	
Other	3	2	0	2	0	0

Notes

1. Full immersion in CAT tools would require translators to use either online projects (e.g., in Memsource) or translation packages (a combination of the source document, TM, TB, and potential context data) by the LSP. This way a freelancer does the translating while the LSP can review the translation in the same format with no need to import the translation, TM, and TB manually into their system. See more in Kornacki (2018).
2. It has to be noted that CAT non-users are both former CAT users who can support those claims with their own experience, as well as freelancers who have never used CAT tools before and, therefore, their views are based on second-hand opinions.

Reference

Kornacki, Michał. (2018). *Computer-assisted Translation (CAT) Tools in the Translator Training Process*. Berlin: Peter Lang.

7 Discussion

Overview of the Chapter

The findings of the study demonstrate current trends in the application of CAT tools in freelance translation. Considering the widespread popularity of CAT tools on the Polish translation market, the results come as slightly surprising since both groups of respondents show many similarities but also important differences (section 7.1). This chapter summarises and discusses the findings outlined in chapter 6, focusing on the reluctance to use CAT technology (section 7.2) due to such factors as technical difficulties (e.g., workflow, user settings), relevance (the use of CAT tools may prove to be time-inefficient in certain conditions), and psychological conditions (technological anxiety). What is more, the chapter discusses the implications of the study for translator training (section 7.3) (e.g., developing technological flexibility and preparing for CAT technology-related changes on the translation market in the future). Finally, the chapter outlines the implications for software developers (section 7.4) in order to promote the means to make the software more user-friendly and easier to use.

7.1 Research Findings

Over two-thirds of all the respondents are aged below 50. Therefore, it can be claimed that the translator population in Poland is rather young. At the same time, over two-thirds of translators report they have at least ten years of work experience in the profession. Those facts lead to the assumption that the number of CAT users (almost 64%) may be a potential result of the age and experience of the population. The data suggest that younger people, with less work experience, were more drawn to it. On the other hand, people aged 60+ were least inclined to use it.

Both groups of respondents do not differ significantly in terms of the languages they use at work. However, it is worth noting that CAT non-users less frequently use English (49% vs 79%) and more frequently use Russian (17.6%), French (15.7%), and Italian (9.8%). By default, CAT tools can be used to translate any language; therefore, the language distribution is rather unlikely to be affected by CAT tools. This claim is supported by the fact that English is the dominant language in both groups (49% to 79%). However, a conclusion can be drawn here that translators working with languages other than English may have difficulty using CAT tools, for instance, because of the language settings in which the user interface (UI) is displayed. The language can usually be selected by the user, but not every CAT tool is available in the preferred language of the translator (for instance, Memsource does not offer the Polish language). The reluctance to use CAT tools can, therefore, be caused by the fact that some translators work in language pairs that are not available in language preferences to be determined for display in the software. The problem is more likely to have been similar in countries where English is not the most spoken language. A much greater sample would have to be analysed in order to determine the actual tool-language dependencies; it would, however, be interesting to devote more attention in future research to the reasons for not using the tools typical for different nations (see section 7.2).

The data collected from the respondents indicate the usefulness of CAT tools in the situation when translation is the main source of income. Seventy-five per cent of CAT users live off translation, whereas in the case of CAT non-users the number is 41%. This tendency suggests that CAT tools enable translators to translate more and, therefore, support themselves financially based only on translation services.

When it comes to the type of documents that constitute the basis of translation jobs, the results are hardly surprising. In the case of orders carried out by CAT users, nearly half of the documents to be translated are editable. In the case of CAT non-users, only 25% of the content is editable. They mostly work on non-editable documents (49%) and do not receive translation packages. The data confirm the assumption that the choice of whether to use CAT tools or not is much simpler for those translators whose jobs involve editable documents as opposed to those translators who deal predominantly with non-editable ones, which would require time and effort to prepare them for CAT tools. The conclusion is further supported by the fact that 29% of CAT non-users have tried using the tools before but, it seems, they have not found them worth the time and money in the context of the translation jobs they do daily.

An interesting fact is that while 49.8% of the CAT users reported the use of more than one tool in their work, 30% of CAT users feel the need to use several different tools. It is no surprise that SDL Trados Studio is the most frequently used CAT tool on the market, mostly thanks to its quality and position on the market (see Kornacki, 2018: 103). Other choices included Memsource, Across, XTM, MateCat, Open Language Tools, Star Transit, Wordbee, DejaVu, SmartCat, and OmegaT. It should be noted that such tools as Wordbee, Star Transit, SmartCat, and OmegaT are used only along-side other CAT tools (by users who use at least three different tools), serving the role of backup/support tools.

It is quite remarkable that about 91% of respondents actually own the CAT tool they use. The authors assumed that the percentage of "LSP-shared" licences would be greater. However, only every fourth person was granted access to the tool for the duration of the project. Rarely, access is granted for an indefinite period. This may imply that CAT technology is not widespread amongst LSPs in Poland, who rely on the resources owned by freelancers themselves. This is further supported by the fact that only 25% of respondents receive jobs in the form of translation packages, and as much as 43% receive editable text files. The lack of CAT packages shows that the LSPs who commission the jobs do not need (or do not know how) to update their own translation repository and build their own translation resources.

Further still, the data suggest that only 40% of respondents are positive about the quality of resources (TMs, TBs) provided by their clients. Again, this may support the claim that CAT tools are not yet that widespread among LSPs in Poland and, as a result, the LSP side handling of resources leaves much room for improvement. On the technical side, almost 90% of users experienced issues with CAT compatibility (mostly package, TM, and TB) in the past (almost 70% of them frequently). Such problems force the use of the client's CAT tool and discourage competition on the market.

Opinions regarding machine translation and its application in the regu-lar translation are mixed. Many freelancers remain sceptical about its use, believing that MT is of no consequence from the point of view of the profes-sional translator since a human will always translate better than a machine. There is no background to those opinions – the authors believe that they are affected by personal (in)experience with MT and popular knowledge. The authors acknowledge that the data would be more accurate if the ques-tions were directed only to people working with MT on a regular basis (MT post-editors, for example) who have hands-on experience with MT engines. Definitely, it is something to consider in future updates to the study.

Despite the issues mentioned earlier, a vast majority of CAT users con-firm the usefulness of these tools. Ninety per cent of them agree that CAT tools have positively influenced their translation efficiency and that it was a good investment of their time and money. While the data presented in Figure 6.1 shows that the average remuneration in both groups is mostly the same, the CAT users have reported a boost to their total income. The fact is more closely related to the volume of text that can be translated using CAT tools (as opposed to regular translation) rather than the change in rate per word/per page.

CAT users appreciate the software because it helps to assure consistency of translation, speeds up the translation process, and allows the user to manage terminology effectively. Seventy-five per cent of them denied the claim that the software results in repeatability of translations and negatively affects the development of translator skills. It is interesting to note, however, that 40% of CAT non-users claim otherwise, which may be the reason why they never used CAT tools or decided to stop using them. The authors assumed that respondents would support the claim that CAT software necessitates text segmentation, which may have a negative effect on the style of the translation. The data show that it is not so – only about 30% of users started to notice the problem.

In general, CAT users are more positive about CAT tools, which may result from their conscious choice and realistic expectations regarding the software. They recognise the advantages and claim that the software does exactly what it was designed to do. However, first-hand experience is necessary to evaluate its strengths and weaknesses, and decide whether it will be useful in the case of a particular translator. The choice of CAT tools is conditioned by several factors (however, about half of the respondents indicated only one reason). The most frequent factor behind the choice of whether to use CAT tools or not was one's own decision, followed by the client's requirement and the opinions of other translators. On the other hand, Table 6.11 presents that the use of CAT software was most often prevented by the coexistence of several factors, including the high price with no customer demand, in particular. Most frequently, however, CAT non-users complain that CAT software is expensive and complicated to use.

7.2　Reluctance to Use CAT Technology

The full range of translation technology cannot be considered universally useful to all translators because of a number of reasons, such as "the file formats that translators are dealing with, the language pair in question, and the quality levels expected, to name just a few" (Kenny and Doherty, 2014: 277). However, there are still a lot of professional translators who do not benefit from CAT technology, although it would be profitable for them to make use of certain tools so as to remain competitive. It has been illustrated that the limited usage of computer-assisted translation in Poland stems mainly from a number of factors other than the apparent unadjustedness of CAT tools in certain areas of translation. One of the reasons for the reluctance to use computer-assisted translation tools is the fear of not having enough knowledge or ability to use all the seemingly complex technological features and services.

Another cause of the reluctance may be a possible problem with the unavailability of the CAT tool in the preferred language. The natural language for UI today is, obviously, English. While most CAT developers offer their systems in other languages,[1] not all of them are available. In fact, the study has shown that some non-users perceive CAT tools as difficult to use. If combined with the fact that not all languages are supported in the UI, it produces a belief that they are not user-friendly, and any attempt at "taming" them may result in the loss of time and money. The data gathered during the study suggest that many translators stop at the general impression stage, not advancing to the actual use stage. If they did, they would see that this is not the case – that CAT tools can be friendly, provided that one chooses the right tool to start. It needs to be recognised that CAT tools are very complex systems which combine lots of features in order to assist the translator. While the general mechanics behind each CAT tool are the same (TM, TB, and MT are used to facilitate the translation process), they differ internally (something a regular user does not see) and, above all, externally (something a regular user sees in the user interface). In this respect, some tools look (and are) more complex than others (e.g., SDL Trados Studio vs memoQ vs Memsource). It is our personal opinion that some UIs are unnecessarily complex and, as a result, may act as deterrents for individual people considering moving to CAT tools.

All those elements add up and result in increased technological anxiety among CAT non-users, especially in the case of older translators. Seldom is it acknowledged that learning the basics of CAT-based translation and CAT tool handling makes it much easier to start using (or migrate altogether to) another CAT tool. UI and language are barriers that can be overcome, provided one does not lose their spirit at the very beginning. Therefore, it is important to start with a CAT tool that offers basic features and functionality over a user-friendly UI, being powerful enough to enable the user to run their everyday jobs at an advanced level once they become familiar with the system.

It needs to be emphasised that only regular use can lead to software fluency which allows for easy and natural use of a given type of software, not necessarily a given computer programme but rather a family of programmes as a whole (in this particular case, CAT tools). The more the translator uses a CAT tool, the easier it is to get the job done, to find and use new (more advanced) features, or to facilitate future work. CAT tools utilise the same basic operating principles and use the same types of resources (albeit incompatible between different tools in their default state). Learning one tool intimately allows the translator to transfer those skills to another CAT environment and start using another tool, if such is the demand.

On the other hand, if a CAT tool is used only occasionally, software fluency is low and deteriorates over time due to lack of practice. A translator who is not fluent in the use of a given CAT tool may suffer from some form of technological anxiety or fear of (mis)handling the software (see section 4.5.3). It was mentioned briefly in comments from the respondents to the study, who suggested to teach students how to handle file extensions, archives, drive partitioning, file transfer protocols, and so on. A successful translator today has to handle all that and more. Add CAT tools to the equation (arguably the most sophisticated type of software in a translator's workshop), and we can clearly see the potential for anxiety.

Another reason for the apparent unwillingness to use CAT tools is the linguistic and cultural nature of the discipline in which the translator most commonly works. In literary or marketing translation, the use of computer-assisted translation can barely be effective. Taking into consideration the characteristics of certain translation areas which do not allow for automated machine-like workflow, the issue in question is not whether to use translation technology but how and when to use it efficiently.

Therefore, it is important to understand the pros and cons of the software in order to assess its relevance to the individual needs of a translator. CAT tools are particularly useful when it comes to texts with content that is repetitive across a range of documents. While CAT technology can be used to translate original texts, like literature, the efficiency of such actions would be questionable (due to the lack of repetitions, text segmentation potentially affecting the bigger picture, or the risk of translating different texts in a similar fashion). In fact, the "segmentation" argument is supported by the study – a number of respondents agreed that, in the case of CAT tools, text segmentation is an issue that could be especially visible in the case of literary translation. Only by understanding the nature of CAT tools and their strengths can translators make proper use of them.

7.3   Implications for Translator Training

Using CAT technology requires a certain amount of perseverance and a great deal of practice. When students are granted an opportunity to not only learn about CAT tools, but more importantly to actually use them in the translation classroom, they become less reluctant to use them. As students acquire more and more knowledge of the tools' functions, they gradually become more likely to make use of advanced translation technology in their professional life. TT interaction (see section 2.2) can be very demanding for translation trainees, so it seems invaluable to have classes directly concerned with the challenges of using CAT tools on a daily basis.

Trainee translators tend to be willing to use CAT tools in the translation classroom but, at the same time, they often seem overwhelmed with technical issues and interaction with translation technology. It is not uncommon for trainees to be daunted when asked to take a scanned document and recreate it in an editable format (like DOCX, for instance) so as to prepare it for translation. Some of them get discouraged and say that they want to become translators, not IT specialists. Given that BA and MA students are most interested in "financial and business aspects of the translation professions" (Pym and Torres-Simón, 2016: 16), it needs to be acknowledged that the contemporary translator is no longer a mere linguist or researcher but a language service provider with advanced technological skills. Therefore, the translator training process cannot be static – it has to be dynamic and evolve together with changing trends on the market (Kornacki, 2018). Trainee translators will benefit substantially from overcoming technological challenges and getting ready to provide a complete translation service which, depending on the project, may involve activities other than mere translation.

What seems crucial here is acknowledging that machine translation and artificial intelligence are indeed capable of taking over the majority of tedious duties of the translator. As Vieira (2018) observes, there is a gap between translation studies and the translation industry as to the competences and roles of the translator:

> on the one hand, the industry might be fit to diagnose and address these issues as and when they appear (e.g., where client satisfaction is affected). On the other hand, the onus is also arguably on those with linguistic expertise and professional translation qualifications to raise awareness of what the role of the translator should encompass.

It is, therefore, of primary importance for translation teachers to make sure their students know how to handle the results of machine translation and how to post-edit the results efficiently.

Revising and evaluating the results of machine translation involves different strategies from a regular revision of translations performed by peer translators or peer trainees. Proper post-editing involves more resources and takes longer than the traditional revision, so the rules of revising MT output vary to a great extent from the strategies usually taught in the translation classroom. It needs to be taken into consideration in the process of translator training that post-editing is going to be predominant in the nearest future, and it must be implemented in translation studies programmes. What is crucial here is how new technological tools are incorporated into the translation curriculum. As Kenny and Doherty (2014: 290) notice, "the adoption of such tools should not force translators into roles that they may find so limiting as to no longer be interesting or professionally rewarding." This is why the authors advocate a pro-active, holistic approach to the teaching and learning of machine translation, in which the translator has a lot of control and critical understanding.

Given that CAT technology changes the whole nature of professional translation services, it needs to be acknowledged that it indeed requires changes in translation education. Although there are barriers that need to be overcome, such as technological anxiety, ethical issues, technical problems, and cognitive friction, such actions aim at giving translation trainees greater efficacy and empowerment.

7.4 Implications for Translation Software Developers

The study has shown that CAT technology prevails among the younger group of respondents. This division may stem from a number of factors, but the most compelling reason is the reported technological anxiety of the translators who do not use CAT tools at all. As was discussed before (see section 4.5.3), many people feel anxious about using new technology – especially given the complexity of CAT tools – and frequently refrain from using it on that ground only. While it cannot be generalised that it does not concern younger translators, it can be observed that this group of respondents grew up in a more technology-oriented environment and had access to computers and the Internet in their childhood or teen years (starting with people born in the late 1970s who had access to reasonably priced personal computers [e.g., IBM PC/AT 286, 386, and so on] and word processors). It is of note that translation as we know it today (with online repositories, fast sharing of data, and so on) became possible with the popularisation of the Internet, which can be associated with Bill Gates's memo to his executive staff (1995), which sent Microsoft in a new direction, made the Internet its top priority, and sped up its popularisation. This timeframe shows that some of the respondents had already worked as translators when those changes were taking place and might have missed the chance to have access to it in the education process. If they were successful without the need for modern technology, as a result, they might not feel that they need it now.

The role of the translation software developers in this instance is to acknowledge the diversity of age and technological flexibility of translators, and promote the software with regard to their age and computer literacy. It could be achieved in a number of ways (e.g., targeted advertising or training videos). However, the first thing that needs to be implemented is showing them why it is worth using CAT tools in everyday work. Again, there are many possibilities to achieve that, one of them being the organisation of free symposiums or training sessions during which an expert would show a given brand of software with all its advantages and then answer critical questions. Such an introductory workshop provides those translators who did not have the opportunity to enrol in a course on translation technology with an opportunity to make up for any loss in the education process and gain the necessary background that we call a technological toolkit (see section 3.3) to further explore CAT technology on their own.

It is vital that such training options be free of change since translators who do not know the tool may not be willing to spend money on supplemental training that they most probably feel no need to attend. It should be mentioned here that, to many translators, the cost of CAT tools is relatively high, especially when coupled with additional paid courses. The role of the expert who conducts the training would be to show the translators the actual cost in terms of time saved and additional income resulting from the characteristics of CAT-based translation.

Additionally, it would probably be best if the introductory training is followed by two more promotional actions. The first one would be to offer translators a fully featured test version of the CAT tool to try it out. Some developers do offer test versions (e.g., Atril offers the full version of Déjà Vu X3 for 30 days, Kilgray offers the full version of memoQ for 45 days, while Memsource is available in a limited mode for an indefinite period of time). While such policies are to be commended, it has to be understood that in the case of a translation professional living off translation, 30 days may be sufficient to learn how to use the software but not to appreciate its benefits in the long run. It would be unprofessional to test the software on actual projects and risk a loss of data or failed deadline because of mishandling the CAT tool. Therefore, a test translation will probably be conducted outside regular translation projects, and more time to appreciate the software may be necessary. It has to be acknowledged, however, that such a policy could be abused, so its pros and cons would have to be considered by the developers.

Another action that could be implemented is to create comprehensive training materials for translators. Many companies at the moment offer online courses (either free access or post-purchase) which can be considered "comprehensive sets of resources that allow to prepare a translator to use the software at a fairly advanced level" (Kornacki, 2018: 134). However, it may not be enough for those professionals who feel increased technological anxiety (see section 4.5.3), as they may find those courses too brief and limited. Detailed videos which present how to access and utilise selected features of CAT tools, coupled with downloadable training materials (translation files, termbase source materials, translation memories, and so on), allow CAT trainees not only to learn how to use the software on actual examples (by following the video step by step) but also to create a point of reference that they can go back to when in doubt during the actual translation process. Detailed and properly named videos can, therefore, help overcome the cognitive friction caused by technology-related problems that occur in the process.

Obviously enough, the prospect of creating a series of detailed videos may seem a daunting challenge for any company, but the competition on the CAT market has been growing steadily in recent years. Developers are updating their products, adding (or moving to) cloud services, and any set of video materials would quickly become obsolete. Nevertheless, the authors believe that in most cases the changes occurring in the case of a particular tool are not that dramatic as they mostly involve the user interface or the efficiency of the software. What we experience at the moment can be described as evolution, not revolution. Developers focus on making current features more effective rather than adding new ones. As a result, the training materials would have to be updated, but probably not that frequently, so – taking into account their undeniable marketing value – a detailed video tutorial approach seems justifiable.

Note

1. For example, Memsource's UI is in English (UK and US) by default; however, users can choose from Chinese, Czech, Danish, Dutch, Finnish, French, German, Greek, Italian, Japanese, Korean, Portuguese, Russian, Slovak, Spanish, and Turkish (via Community Translation).

References

Gates, Bill. (1995). *The Internet Tidal Wave*. Internal Company Communication, 26 May 1995. Available at: www.sindark.com/genre/1995-The-Internet-Tidal-Wave.pdf (Accessed: 27 June 2019).

Kenny, Dorothy and Doherty, Stephen. (2014). Statistical Machine Translation in the Translation Curriculum: Overcoming Obstacles and Empowering Translators. *The Interpreter and Translator Trainer*, vol. 8(2), pp. 276–294.

Kornacki, Michał. (2018). *Computer-assisted Translation (CAT) Tools in the Translator Training Process*. Berlin: Peter Lang.

Pym, Anthony and Torres-Simón, Esther. (2016). Designing a Course in Translation Studies to Respond to Students' Questions. *The Interpreter and Translator Trainer*, vol. 10(2), pp. 183–203. https://doi.org/10.1080/1750399X.2016.1198179

Vieira, Lucas Nunes. (2018). Automation Anxiety and Translators. *Translation Studies*, https://doi.org/10.1080/14781700.2018.1543613

8 Conclusion

The present study has raised questions about the nature of using CAT tools in freelance translation. The authors discussed the typology of translator-technology interaction and its impact on the translation workflow. The book examines the issue of anxiety in freelance translation experienced by translators confronted with technological issues. Given that the use of technology exerts a significant impact on the translation process, the book also examines the adverse effect of CAT technology on the translator's cognitive and metacognitive skills.

To illustrate current trends and practices in the application of CAT tools, the authors discuss the findings of the exploratory study on freelance translators in Poland, conducted using the CAWI technique. Their attitudes towards the study are analysed prior to the discussion of the results since the comments of the participants shed some light on their perception of the profession, their role on the translation market, and their view on academia.

The results of the study have been processed using SPSS statistics software. The data revealed a considerable reluctance of translators to use CAT tools in freelance translation. These findings show that freelance translators choose CAT tools based predominantly on their own needs rather than on external requirements (although the client's requirement is the second most common answer). At the same time, the study has shown that CAT tools are more likely to be chosen by younger translators, which the authors of the book associate with lower technological anxiety in this group of professionals (see sections 4.5.3 and 7.2). However, the data also suggest that the choice of whether to use or not use CAT tools is directly related to the format of the documents for translation – translators working predominantly with scanned text and complex PDF files are less likely to use CAT tools.

A correlation may be drawn between job type, market distribution, and individual income distribution for each translator. The data show that translation is the main source of income for 74.4% of CAT users and only for 41.2% of CAT non-users. This tendency shows that translators choose CAT tools when they want to translate more words per day in order to earn enough money to support themselves financially. They do not want to waste time on documents which need considerable time and effort to be appropriated to the CAT environment. However, this is not an issue for those translators who consider translation a second (or odd) job, thus filling the void left by CAT users in the translation market. Again, an additional study would be required to narrow some of the results and study the influence of technological anxiety on job preference. The data gained this way would answer the fundamental question regarding the extent to which technology shapes translation as a profession. In fact, given the rapid advances of translation technology, it would be an interesting avenue for further research to find out what discourages translators from making use of its benefits in other countries and how to address this issue within translator training.

The data collected and analysed in the course of the study show that, despite the continuous growth and advancement of translation technology, there is still a great number of professional translators who refrain from using CAT tools or fail to use them efficiently and do not make use of all the features available to better address their clients' expectations. The study was conducted in the belief that it is important to conduct continuous surveys on professional translators to assess the current shape of the translation market, adapt the software to the current market needs, and improve teaching programmes. The findings of the study helped to identify the needs of the market and suggest some implications for software developers, translator trainers, and other language industry stakeholders.

References

Alcina, Amparo. (2008). Translation Technologies Scope, Tools and Resources. *Target*, vol. 20(1), pp. 79–102. https://doi.org/10.1075/target.20.1.05alc

Allen, Mike. (2017). *The Sage Encyclopedia of Communication Research Methods*. Vols. 1–4. Thousand Oaks, CA: SAGE Publications, Inc. https://doi.org/10.4135/9781483381411

Automatic Language Processing Advisory Committee (ALPAC). (1966). *Language and Machines. Computers in Translation and Linguistics*. Washington, DC: National Academy of Sciences. Available at: www.mt-archive.info/ALPAC-1966.pdf (accessed: 25 March 2019).

Autor, David H. (2015). Why Are There Still So Many Jobs? The History and Future of Workplace Automation. *Journal of Economic Perspectives*, vol. 29(3), pp. 3–30.

Bahdanau, Dzmitry, Cho, Kyunghyun and Yoshua, Bengio. (2014). *Neural Machine Translation by Jointly Learning to Align and Translate* [Online]. Available at: https://arxiv.org/pdf/1409.0473.pdf (Accessed: 31 May 2020).

Bandura, Albert. (1992). Self-efficacy Mechanism in Human Agency. *American Psychologist*, vol. 37, pp. 122–147.

Bandura, Albert. (1994). Self-efficacy. In: Ramachaudran, V. S. (ed.), *Encyclopedia of Human Behavior*. Vol. 4. New York: Academic Press, pp. 71–81 (Reprinted in Friedman, H. [ed.], *Encyclopedia of Mental Health*. San Diego: Academic Press, 1998).

Bandura, Albert. (2009). Cultivate Self-efficacy for Personal and Organizational Effectiveness. In: Locke, E. A. (ed.), *Handbook of Principles of Organization Behavior*. 2nd ed. New York: Wiley, pp. 179–200.

Bar-Hillel, Yehoshua. (1960). *The Present Status of Automatic Translation of Languages: Advances in Computers*. Vol. 1 [Online]. Available at: www.mt-archive.info/Bar-Hillel-1960.pdf (Accessed: 27 August 2019).

Bartholomew, David J. (2015). Factor Analysis and Latent Structure Analysis: Overview. In Wright, James D. (ed.), *International Encyclopedia of the Social & Behavioral Sciences*. 2nd ed. Amsterdam: Elsevier, pp. 691–697.

Bartlett, Maurice S. (1937). Properties of Sufficiency and Statistical Tests. Proceedings of the Royal Statistical Society, Series A (160). *Mathematical and Physical Sciences*. Vol. 160, No. 901, May 18, 1937, pp. 268–282. JSTOR 96803 (https://jstor.org/stable/96803)

Bell, Roger. (1991). *Translation and Translating: Theory and Practice*. London: Longman.

Bentivogli, Luisa, Bertoldi, Nicola, Cettolo, Mauro, Federico, Marcello, Negri, Matteo and Turchi, Marco. (2016). On the Evaluation of Adaptive Machine Translation for Human Post-Editing. *IEEE/ACM Transactions on Audio, Speech, and Language Processing*, vol. 24(2), pp. 388–399. https://doi.org/10.1109/TASLP.2015.2509241

Bogucki, Łukasz. (2019). *Areas and Methods of Audiovisual Translation Research*. 3rd revised ed. Berlin: Peter Lang.

Bogucki, Łukasz and Deckert, Mikołaj (eds.). (2020). *Handbook of Audiovisual Translation and Media Accessibility*. Basingstoke: Palgrave Macmillan.

Bowker, Lynne. (2002). *Computer-aided Translation Technology: A Practical Instruction*. Ottawa: University of Ottawa Press.

Bowker, Lynne. (2005). Productivity vs Quality? A Pilot Study on the Impact of Translation Memory Systems. *Localisation Focus*, vol. 4(1), pp. 13–20.

Brosnan, Mark. (1998). *Technophobia, the Psychological Impact of Information Technology*. New York, NY: Routledge.

Brosnan, Mark and Davidson, Marylin J. (1996). Psychological Gender Issues in Computing. *Journal of Gender, Work and Organization*, vol. 3(1), pp. 13–25.

Bundgaard, Kristine. (2017). Translator Attitudes Towards Translator-Computer Interaction – Findings from a Workplace Study. *HERMES-Journal of Language and Communication in Business*, pp. 125–144.

Bundgaard, Kristine, Christensen, Tina P. and Schjoldager, Anne. (2016). Translator-Computer Interaction in Action: An Observational Process Study of Computer-aided Translation. *Journal of Specialised Translation*, vol. 25, pp. 106–130.

Chan, Sin-Wei. (2004). *A Dictionary of Translation Technology*. Hong Kong: The Chinese University Press.

Chan, Sin-Wei. (2012). *Translation Technology: Past, Present and Future*. Paper presented at the 2012 LTTC International Conference: The Making of a Translator, Taipei.

Cronin, Michael. (2013). *Translation in the Digital Age*. London and New York: Routledge.

CSA. (2019). *The Largest Language Service Providers: 2019* [Online]. Available at: https://csa-research.com/More/Global-Market-Study/Top-100-LSPs (Accessed: 9 July 2019).

DePalma, Donald A. (2012). *Translation Future Shock*, pp. 16–18 [Private access per subscription. https://csa-research.com]. (Accessed: 9 July 2019).

DePalma, Donald A., Pielmeier, Hélène and O'Mara, Paul D. (2019). *The Language Services Market: 2019. 15th Annual Review of the Services and Technology Industry That Supports Translation, Localization, and Interpreting* [Private access per subscription. https://csa-research.com]. (Accessed: 9 July 2019).

Doherty, Stephen. (2016). The Impact of Translation Technologies on the Process and Product of Translation. *International Journal of Communication*, vol. 10, pp. 947–969. http://doi.org/10.1177/001316446002000116

Ehrensberger-Dow, Maureen and Massey, Gary. (2014). *Constraints on Creativity: The Case of CAT Tools* [Online]. Available at: www.researchgate.net/publication/

278676021_Constraints_on_creativity_The_case_of_CAT_tools (Accessed: 24 July 2019).

Ehrensberger-Dow, Maureen and O'Brien, Sharon. (2015). Ergonomics of the Translation Workplace: Potential for Cognitive Friction. *Translation Spaces*, vol. 4(1), pp. 98–118.

EMT Expert Group. (2009). *Competences for Professional Translators, Experts in Multilingual and Multimedia Communication*. Brussels: European Commission.

EMT Expert Group. (2017). *Competence Framework 2017* [Online]. Available at: https://ec.europa.eu/info/sites/info/files/emt_competence_fwk_2017_en_web. pdf (Accessed: 3 January 2020).

Enríquez Raído, Vanessa and Austermühl, Frank. (2003). Translation, Localization, and Technology: Current Developments. In: Gonzalez, Luis P. (ed.), *Speaking in Tongues: Language Across Contexts and Users*. València: Publicacions de la Universitat de València, pp. 225–250.

Esselink, Bert. (2003). *The Evolution of Localization. Guide to Localization. Multilingual Computing and Technology*. Archived from the original on 2012–09–07 [Online]. Available at: https://web.archive.org/web/20120907235057/http://isg. urv.es/library/papers/Esselink_Evolution.pdf (Accessed: 4 October 2019).

Fantinuoli, Claudio. (2018). *Interpreting and Technology: The Upcoming Technological Turn*. Berlin: Language Science Press.

Farina, Francisca, Arce, Ramon, Sobral, Jorge and Carames, Rosa. (1991). Predictors of Anxiety Towards Computers. *Computers in Human Behaviour*, vol. 7(4), pp. 263–267.

Garcia, Ignacio. (2015). Computer-aided Translation Systems. In: Chan, Sin-wei (ed.), *Routledge Encyclopedia of Translation Technology*. Amsterdam and Philadelphia: Routledge, pp. 68–87.

Gates, Bill. (1995). *The Internet Tidal Wave*. Internal Company Communication, 26 May 1995. Available at: www.sindark.com/genre/1995-The-Internet-Tidal-Wave. pdf (Accessed: 27 June 2019).

Georgeon, Olivier and Ritter, Frank E. (2012). An Intrinsically-Motivated Schema Mechanism to Model and Simulate Emergent Cognition. *Cognitive Systems Research*, vol. 15–16, pp. 73–92.

Gil, José R. B. and Pym, Anthony. (2006). Technology and Translation (a Pedagogical Overview). In: Pym, Anthony, Perekrestenko, Alexander and Starink, Bram (eds.), *Translation Technology and Its Teaching (With Much Mention of Localization)*. Intercultural Studies Group, Tarragona and Reus: Universitat Rovira i Virgili, pp. 5–19. ISBN: 978-84-611-1131-2

Gilbert, David, Lee-Kelley, Liz and Barton, Maya. (2003). Technophobia, Gender Influences and Consumer Decision-Making for Technology-Related Products. *European Journal of Innovation Management*, vol. 6(4), pp. 253–263.

Goldberg, Yoav. (2017). *Neural Network Methods in Natural Language Processing (Synthesis Lectures on Human Language Technologies)*. San Rafael, CA: Morgan & Claypool.

González Davies, Maria. (2004). *Multiple Voices in the Translation Classroom*. Amsterdam and Philadelphia: John Benjamins.

Goodfellow, Ian, Bengio, Yoshua and Courville, Aaron. (2016). *Deep Learning (Adaptive Computation and Machine Learning Series)*. Cambridge, MA: MIT Press.

Göpferich, Susanne. (2009). Towards a Model of Translation Competence and Its Acquisition: The Longitudinal Study Transcomp. In: Göpferich, Susanne, Jakobsen, Arne L. and Mees, Ingrid M. (eds.), *Behind the Mind: Methods, Models and Results in Translation Process Research*. Copenhagen: Samfundslitteratur Press, pp. 11–37.

Gouadec, Daniel. (2007). *Translation as a Profession*. Amsterdam and Philadelphia: John Benjamins.

Haro-Soler, Maria and Kiraly, Don. (2019). Exploring Self-efficacy Beliefs in Symbiotic Collaboration with Students: An Action Research Project. *The Interpreter and Translator Trainer*, vol. 13(3), pp. 255–270. www.researchgate.net/publication/278676021_Constraints_on_creativity_The_case_of_CAT_tools (Accessed: 24 July 2019).

Hurtado Albir, Amparo. (2007). Competence-based Curriculum Design for Training Translators. *The Interpreter and Translator Trainer*, vol. 1(2), pp. 163–195.

Hutchins, John. (1997). Translation Technology and the Translator. In: Greensmith, Catherine and Vandamme, Marilyn (eds.), *ITI Conference 11. Proceedings [of] International Conference, Exhibition & AGM*. London: Institute of Translation & Interpreting, pp. 113–120.

Hutchins, John. (1999). *Compendium of Translation Software* [Online]. Available at: www.hutchinsweb.me.uk/Compendium.htm (Accessed: 16 July 2019).

Hutchins, John. (2010). Machine Translation: A Concise History. *Journal of Translation Studies*, vol. 13(1–2), pp. 29–70.

Hutchins, John and Somers, Harold. (1992). *An Introduction to Machine Translation*. London: Academic Press Ltd.

IBM. (2012). *How-to Guide for IBM® SPSS® Statistics Software* [Online]. Available at: https://methods.sagepub.com/dataset/howtoguide/kmo-nilt-2012 (Accessed: 16 February 2020).

Igbaria, Magid and Chakrabarti, Alogk. (1990). Computer Anxiety and Attitudes Towards Microcomputer Use. *Behaviour & Information Technology*, vol. 9(3), pp. 229–241.

Kaiser, Henry F. (1960). The Application of Electronic Computers to Factor Analysis. *Educational and Psychological Measurement*, vol. 20, pp. 141–151.

Kanyongo, Gibbs Y. (2005). Determining the Correct Number of Components to Extract From a Principal Components Analysis: A Monte Carlo Study of the Accuracy of the Scree Plot. *Journal of Modern Applied Statistical Methods*, vol. 4(1), pp. 120–133.

Kenny, Dorothy and Doherty, Stephen. (2014). Statistical Machine Translation in the Translation Curriculum: Overcoming Obstacles and Empowering Translators. *The Interpreter and Translator Trainer*, vol. 8(2), pp. 276–294.

Kiraly, Don. (1995). *Pathways to Translation: Pedagogy and Process*. Kent: Kent State University Press.

Kiraly, Don. (2000). *A Social Constructivist Approach to Translator Education: Empowerment from Theory to Practice*. Manchester: St Jerome.

Kiraly, Don. (2014). From Assumptions About Knowing and Learning to Praxis in Translator Education. In: Piotrowska, Maria and Tyupa, Sergiy (eds.), *Challenges in Translation Pedagogy, Special Issue of Intralinea* [Online]. Available at: www. intralinea.org/specials/article/2100 (Accessed: 17 December 2019).

Klimkowska, Katarzyna (2013). *Orientacja na sukces zawodowy studentów kończących studia translatorskie.* Lublin: UMCS.

Klimkowski, Konrad. (2015). *Towards a Shared Curriculum in Translator and Interpreter Education.* Wrocław and Washington, DC: WSF, PAN and International Communicology Institute.

Kornacki, Michał. (2018). *Computer-assisted Translation (CAT) Tools in the Translator Training Process.* Berlin: Peter Lang.

LaMorte, Wayne W. (2017). *Mann Whitney U Test (Wilcoxon Rank Sum Test).* Boston: University School of Public Health [Online]. Available at: http://sphweb.bumc.bu.edu/otlt/mph-modules/bs/bs704_nonparametric/BS704_Nonparametric4.html (Accessed: 16 February 2020).

Latham, Gary P., Winters, Dawn C. and Locke, Edwin A. (1994). Cognitive and Motivational Effects of Participation: A Mediator Study. *Journal of Organizational Behavior*, vol. 15, pp. 49–63. https://doi.org/10.1002/job.4030150106

Locke, Edwin A. and Latham, Gary P. (2002). Building a Practically Useful Theory of Goal Setting and Task Motivation. *American Psychologist*, vol. 57(9), pp. 705–717.

Melby, Alan. (1982). Multi-level Translation Aids in a Distributed System. In Horecký, Jan (ed.), *Proceedings of Coling 1982.* Amsterdam: North Holland.

Melby, Alan. (1994). The Translator Workstation. In: Hammond, Deanna L. (ed.), *Professional Issues for Translators and Interpreters.* American Translators Association Scholarly Monograph Series VII. Amsterdam/Philadelphia: John Benjamins, pp. 127–149.

Melby, Alan. (1998). *Eight Types of Translation Technology* [Online]. Available at www.ttt.org/technology/8types.pdf (Accessed: 16 July 2019).

Mell, Peter and Grance, Timothy. (2011). *The NIST Definition of Cloud Computing* Gaithersburg: National Institute of Standards and Technology: U.S. Department of Commerce [Online]. Available at: https://nvlpubs.nist.gov/nistpubs/Legac SP/nistspecialpublication800-145.pdf (Accessed: 21 July 2019).

memoQ. (2020). CAT Tool Developed by Kilgray, Budapest, Hungary.

Memsource. (2019). *Memsource Translate* [Online]. Available at: www.memsourc com/features/memsource-translate/ (Accessed: 21 July 2019).

Moorkens, Joss. (2017). Under Pressure: Translation in Times of Austerity. *Perspectives Studies in Translatology*, vol. 25(3), pp. 464–477.

Mossop, Brian. (2006). Has Computerization Changed Translation? *META*, v. 51(4), pp. 1–9. https://doi.org/10.7202/014342ar

Muñoz Martín, Ricardo. (2014). Situating Translation Expertise: A Review with a Sketch of a Construct. In: Schwieter, John and Ferreira, Aline (eds.), *The Development of Translation Competence: Theories and Methodologies from Psycholinguistics and Cognitive Science.* Cambridge: Cambridge Scholars Publishing, pp. 2–54.

Nagao, Makoto. (1981). A Framework of a Mechanical Translation Between Japanese and English. In: Elithorn, Alick and Banerji, Ranan (eds.), *Artificial nd Human Intelligence: Edited Review Papers Presented at the International NATO*

Symposium on Artificial and Human Intelligence. Amsterdam: Elsevier Science Publishers. B.V., pp. 173–180.

National Institute of Standards and Technology (NIST). (2013). *Correlation Matrix* [Online]. Available at: www.itl.nist.gov/div898/software/dataplot/refman2/auxillar/corrmatr.htm (Accessed: 16 February 2020).

Novović, Miloš. (2017). User-Generated Content: How Broad Licensing Terms Threaten the Web. In: Taddeo, Mariarosaria and Floridi, Luciano (eds.), *The Responsibilities of Online Service Providers*. New York: Springer International Publishing AG, pp. 201–217.

O'Brien, Sharon. (2012). Translation as Human-Computer Interaction. *Translation Spaces*, vol. 1(1), pp. 101–122.

O'Brien, Sharon, Ehrensberger-Dow, Maureen, Hasler, Marcel and Connolly, Megan. (2017). Irritating CAT Tool Features that Matter to Translators. *HERMES-Journal of Language and Communication in Business*, vol. 56, pp. 145–162.

O'Brien, Sharon and Moorkens, Joss. (2014). Towards Intelligent Post-Editing Interfaces. In: Baur, Wolfram, Eichner, Brigitte, Kalina, Sylvia, Keßler, Norma, Mayer, Felix and Ørsted, Jeannette (eds.), *Proceedings* of the XXth *FIT World Congress*. Berlin: Bundesverband der Dolmetscher und Übersetzer e.V., pp. 131–137

Okebukola, Peter and Woda, Augustinus. (1993). The Gender Factor in Computer Anxiety and Interest Among Some Australian High School Students. *Educational Research*, vol. 35(2), pp. 181–189.

PACTE Group. (2003). Building a Translation Competence Model. In: Alves, Fabio (ed.), *Triangulating Translation: Perspectives in Process Oriented Research*. Amsterdam: John Benjamins, pp. 43–65.

PACTE Group. (2005). Investigating Translation Competence: Conceptual and Methodological Issues. *Meta*, vol. 50(2), pp. 609–619.

Piaget, Jean. (1951). *The Psychology of Intelligence*. London: Routledge and Kegan Paul.

Pietrzak, Paulina. (2018). The Effects of Students' Self-regulation on Translation Quality. *Babel: International Journal of Translation*, vol. 64(5/6), pp. 819–839.

Piotrowska, Maria. (2007). *Proces decyzyjny tłumacza. Podstawy metodologii nauczania przekładu pisemnego*. Kraków: Wydawnictwo Naukowe Akademii Pedagogicznej.

Pym, Anthony. (2003). Redefining Translation Competence in an Electronic Age. In Defence of a Minimalist Approach. *META*, vol. XLVIII(4), pp. 481–497.

Pym, Anthony. (2011a). What Technology Does to Translating. *Translation & Interpreting*, vol. 3(1), pp. 1–9.

Pym, Anthony. (2011b). Website Localization. In: Malmkjaer, Kirsten and Windle, Kevin (eds.), *The Oxford Handbook for Translation Studies*. Oxford: Oxford University Press, pp. 410–424.

Pym, Anthony. (2012). Translation Skill-Sets in a Machine-Translation Age. *Meta*, vol. 58(3), pp. 487–503. https://doi.org/10.7202/1025047ar

Pym, Anthony. (2013). Translation Skill-Sets in a Machine-Translation Age. *Meta*, vol. 58(3), pp. 487–503. https://doi.org/10.7202/1025047ar

Pym, Anthony, Grin, François, Sfreddo, Claudio and Chan, Andy L. J. (2012). *The Status of the Translation Profession in the European Union* [Online]. Available at: https://

termcoord.eu/wp-content/uploads/2013/08/The_status_of_the_translation_profession_in_the_European_Union.pdf. (Accessed: 9 July 2019).

Pym, Anthony and Torres-Simón, Esther. (2016). Designing a Course in Translation Studies to Respond to Students' Questions. *The Interpreter and Translator Trainer*, vol. 10(2), pp. 183–203. https://doi.org/10.1080/1750399X.2016.1198179

Rinsche, Adriane and Portera-Zanotti, Nadia. (2009). *Study on the Size of Language Industry in the EU* [Online]. Available at: https://publications.europa.eu/en/publication-detail/-/publication/9a68479a-1c07-4c43-8d1a-8d49782c0808 (Accessed: 9 July 2019).

Risku, Hanna, Pein-Weber, Christina and Milošević, Jelena. (2016). "The Task of the Translator": Comparing the Views of the Client and the Translator. *International Journal of Communication*, vol. 10(2016), pp. 989–1008.

Robinson, Douglas. (1997). *Becoming a Translator: An Accelerated Course*. London: Routledge.

Rodríguez de Céspedes, Begoña. (2017). Addressing Employability and Enterprise Responsibilities in the Translation Curriculum. *The Interpreter and Translator Trainer*, vol. 11(2–3), pp. 107–122. https://doi.org/10.1080/17503 99X.2017.1344816

Rosen, Larry D. and Maguire, Phyllisann. (1990). Myths and Realities of Computerphobia: A Meta-analysis. *Anxiety Research*, vol. 3, pp. 175–191.

Rosen, Larry D., Sears, Deborah C. and Weil, Michelle M. (1993). Treating Technophobia: A Longitudinal Evaluation of the Computerphobia Reduction Program. *Computers in Human Behaviour*, vol. 9, pp. 27–50.

Samuelsson-Brown, Geoffrey. (1996). New Technology for Translators. In: Owens, Rachel (ed.), *The Translator's Handbook*. London: Aslib, pp. 279–293.

Shreve, Gregory M. (2006). The Deliberate Practice: Translation and Expertise. *Journal of Translation Studies*, vol. 9(1), pp. 27–42.

Snedecor, George W. and Cochran, William G. (1989). *Statistical Methods*. 8th ed. Ames: Iowa State University Press.

Somers, Harold. (1999). Review Article: Example-based Machine Translation. *Machine Translation*, vol. 14, pp. 113–158.

Spearman, Charles. (1904). The Proof and Measurement of Association Between Two Things. *American Journal of Psychology*, vol. 15(1), pp. 72–101. https://doi.org/10.2307/1412159

Strandvik, Ingemar. (2017). Evaluation of Outsourced Translations. State of Play in the European Commission's Directorate-General for Translation (DGT). In: Svoboda, Tomáš, Biel, Łucja and Łoboda, Krzysztof (eds.), *Quality Aspects in Institutional Translation*. Berlin: Language Science Press, pp. 123–137. https://doi.org/10.5281/zenodo.1048194

SYSTRAN. (2019). *What Is Machine Translation?* [Online]. Available at: www.systransoft.com/systran/translation-technology/what-is-machine-translation/ (Accessed: 28 August 2019).

Taboga, Marco. (2017). *Lectures on Probability Theory and Mathematical Statistics*. 3rd ed. Scotts Valley, CA: CreateSpace Independent Publishing Platform.

Teixeira, Carlos. (2011). Knowledge of Provenance and Its Effects on Translation Performance. In: Sharp, Bernadette, Zock, Michael and Jakobsen, Arnt Lykke (eds.), *Human-Machine Interaction in Translation*. Frederiksberg: Samfundslitteratur, pp. 107–118.

Tennent, Martha (ed.). (2005). *Training for the New Millennium: Pedagogies for Translation and Interpreting*. Amsterdam and Philadelphia: John Benjamins.

UCLA: Statistical Consulting Group. (2020). *What Does Cronbach's Alpha Mean? UCLA: Statistical Consulting Group* [Online]. Available at: https://stats.idre.ucla.edu/other/mult-pkg/faq/general/faq-how-do-i-cite-web-pages-and-programs-from-the-ucla-statistical-consulting-group/ (Accessed: 16 February 2020).

Vieira, Lucas Nunes. (2018). Automation Anxiety and Translators. *Translation Studies*, https://doi.org/10.1080/14781700.2018.1543613

Wołk, Krzysztof and Marasek, Krzysztof. (2018). Neural-based Machine Translation for Medical Text Domain. Based on European Medicines Agency Leaflet Texts. *Procedia Computer Science*, vol. 64, pp. 2–9.

Wood, Robert and Bandura, Albert. (1989). Impact of Conceptions of Ability on Self-regulatory Mechanisms and Complex Decision Making. *Journal of Personality and Social Psychology*, vol. 56(3), pp. 407–415. https://doi.org/10.1037/0022-3514.56.3.407

Wu, Yonghui, Schuster, Mike, Chen, Zhifeng, Le, Quoc, V., Norouzi, Mohammad, Macherey, Wolfgang, Krikun, Maxim, Cao, Yuan, Gao, Qin, Macherey, Klaus, Klingner, Jeff, Shah, Apurva, Johnson, Melvin, Liu, Xiaobing, Kaiser, Łukasz, Gouws, Stephan, Kato, Yoshikiyo, Kudo, Taku, Kazawa, Hideto, Stevens, Keith, Kurian, George, Patil, Nishant, Wang, Wei, Young, Cliff, Smith, Jason, Riesa, Jason, Rudnick, Alex, Vinyals, Oriol, Corrado, Greg, Hughes, Macduff, and Dean, Jeffrey. (2016). *Google's Neural Machine Translation System: Bridging the Gap Between Human and Machine Translation* [Online]. Available at: https://arxiv.org/pdf/1609.08144.pdf (Accessed: 31 May 2020).

Zaretskaya, Anna, Corpas Pastor, Gloria and Seghiri, Miriam. (2015). Integration of Machine Translation in CAT Tools: State of the Art, Evaluation and User Attitudes. *SKASE Journal for Translation and Interpretation*, vol. 8(1), pp. 76–88.

Index